Praise for

LOST IN THE STREAM

"Movies are to Jeff Rauseo what water is to Aquaman."

—**Brian Levant**, director of *The Flintstones* and *Jingle All the Way*

"The best thing to read besides subtitles on a movie."

—**Chris Collins**, host of *There Are Too Many Movies*

"A mesmerizing deep dive into the history of cinema. Jeff Rauseo unpacks the politics, finances, and creative battles behind the movies we love. From silent films to streaming, it's a must-read for cinephiles. A fascinating, well-researched triumph that captures Hollywood's ever-evolving landscape."

—**Adnan Virk**, film critic and host of *Cinephile*

"A blast from beginning to end, Jeff Rauseo's book is nostalgic and funny and sad in equal measures as it recalls a time of VHS and Blockbusters and days spent lost at the local cinema (all subjects near and dear to my own heart). Jeff writes in the best way possible: honestly and with a clear passion for the world of film, filmmakers, and film lovers. I devoured everything he had to say. Pauline Kael famously 'lost it' at the movies but Jeff Rauseo 'found it' at the movies, and I've now found an author worth watching out for. Looking forward to seeing where he takes us next."

—**Neil LaBute,** director of *Death at a Funeral*

"From latchkey kids raised in the local video store to modern youth who have never known life without the constant deluge of screens, content, and the almighty algorithm, *Lost in the Stream* is a fascinating exploration of the film industry's ongoing evolution. With eloquence and passion, Rauseo speaks directly to the heart of cinephiles."

—**Alex DiVincenzo,** Bloody Disgusting

"Jeff loves movies. Like, every single aspect of them, from how they are made to how we consume them. So, if you love movies that much, too, you'll enjoy this book!"

—**Brandon Dermer,** director

"Just when I needed another reason to fan out about Jeff Rauseo and his enviably encyclopedic movie mind, *Lost in the Stream* comes along..."

—**Josh Ruben,** filmmaker

"Jeff is the best voice in the enthusiast community, and his book shows that in spades. His understanding and appreciation of the human and communal aspects of film, pushing the medium beyond just being referred to as 'content,' is refreshing. His love and respect for the art form, from technical aspects to filmmaking, is passionate and relatable. Every collector and enthusiast needs to give this a read!"

—**Damon Weathers**, physical production manager at Legacy Effects

"Jeff is an invaluable voice in the world of film. His passion and commitment to making movie watching a seamless, meaningful experience is a breath of fresh air in an era dominated by fragmented streaming platforms and convoluted licensing deals that force audiences to chase down the content they love. His infectious enthusiasm for physical media is a powerful reminder that we can take ownership of how we engage with film—beyond the limitations of digital ecosystems. Jeff's deep knowledge of cinema and film history, paired with his drive to spotlight both celebrated and under-the-radar titles, makes him a true advocate for media literacy and thoughtful viewing. I couldn't be more excited to see what he brings to the table with *Lost in the Stream*."

—**Adam Hlavac**, creator of Heroes Reforged

"Film shapes culture, challenges perspectives, and inspires change. Jeff Rauseo explores cinema's profound impact on society, art, and the human experience. Movies aren't just entertainment—they're a reflection of who we are."

—Hunter Rebner, film studies educator at Albert Einstein Academy

LOST

in the

STREAM

Jeff Rauseo

LOST

in the

How Algorithms Redefined the Way
Movies Are Made and Watched

STREAM

mango
PUBLISHING

MIAMI

For permission requests, please contact the publisher at:
Mango Publishing Group
5966 South Dixie Highway, Suite 300
Miami, FL 33143
info@mango.bz

For special orders, quantity sales, course adoptions and corporate sales,
please email the publisher at sales@mango.bz. For trade and wholesale
sales, please contact Ingram Publisher Services at customer.service@
ingramcontent.com or +1.800.509.4887.

Lost in the Stream: How Algorithms Redefined the Way Movies Are
Made and Watched

Library of Congress Cataloging-in-Publication number: requested
ISBN: (p) 978-1-68481-819-8 (e) 978-1-68481-807-5
BISAC: PER004030 PERFORMING ARTS / Film / History & Criticism

Printed in the United States of America

For Sam and Hannah. The joy you bring me each day gives purpose to my work. I hope one day you will look back and think your dad was pretty cool.

TABLE OF CONTENTS

FOREWORD

TABLE OF CONTENTS

It was July 1985. I was five years old. My mom, who worked nights, was home with me during a massive downpour. Stuck with a bored and restless son, she phoned a neighbor, and together we decided to go to the movies. A month earlier, she and I had caught the trailer for *Back to the Future* before *The Goonies*, and it looked awesome. So, off we went to the Triboro Theater in North Attleboro, Massachusetts, to check it out.[1]

In the first minute of this movie, I was transported somewhere else. You know the scene: Marty walks into Doc's lab, plugs in his guitar, cranks every knob to the max. I remember covering my ears, wincing, bracing for the inevitable blast. The film had grabbed me by the collar and pulled me in. Exactly one hour and fifty-six minutes later, when the words "TO BE CONTINUED" appeared on screen, I was breathless. Quite simply, in the five years Michael Mohan had lived on this planet,

---

1   This theater had the stickiest fucking floor of all time. Every time you lifted your foot, there was this loud, rubbery ripping sound. I can still hear it. *Riiip. Riiip. Riiip.*

this moment was the coolest fucking thing he had ever fucking experienced. On the drive home through the rain, I knew: I wanted to spend my life being part of the creation of whatever *that* was.

And so began the lifelong obsession. Every Sunday, I'd steal the arts section from *The Boston Globe*, cut out the movie ads, and tape them to my bedroom walls. I didn't know what a screenplay was, but I filled notebooks with movie ideas. I pored over *Leonard Maltin's Movie Guide* every year until the spine cracked in two. When we finally got a VCR, we'd rent two PG-13-or-less movies every weekend.

In 1993, everything changed—because I could finally see R-rated films (as long as there wasn't nudity). I remember feeling more mature now that my dad was taking me to such adult fare as *In the Line of Fire* (which still rips, by the way). I'd set my VCR to SLP mode and tape late-night movies off Bravo—back when Bravo showed indie films and obscure '70s oddities. That's how I fell in love with *Slacker* and *Heavy*—films that felt like they were made by real people, outside the system. Seeing movies like that gave me hope that maybe this dream of mine wasn't *totally* far-fetched.

Once I could drive, watching movies became a pilgrimage. I'd read in *Premiere* magazine about this strange black-

and-white film called *Pi*, and I had to see it. It wasn't playing anywhere near the suburbs, so I drove to the train station, took the train into Boston, transferred to the red line, got off at MIT, and walked to Kendall Square to catch it on opening weekend. That journey was part of the experience. The anticipation. The chase. It made the movie feel like it belonged to me.

That's why I've always gravitated toward physical media. When I look at my wall of Blu-rays, I don't just see titles—I see identity. I see the stretch where I was obsessed with 1980s romantic comedies. The year I watched every single John Cassavetes film. The months I devoured every mainstream erotic thriller while writing *The Voyeurs*. And now, a new shelf filled with disturbing films like *Testament*, *Combat Shock*, and *Come and See*—movies that, in a fucked-up way, are helping me cope with my mother's illness.

These aren't just objects. They're timestamps. Every time I pass by them, they reinforce my connection—to the films, and to the version of me that watched them.

More and more, they've also become a way to discover new favorites. When someone I trust recommends a film and it's on Blu-ray, I just buy it—sight unseen. That disc becomes a promise to myself to actually sit down and fucking watch it. Recently, that's how I finally ended up checking out *Eyes of Laura Mars*—which is so incredible that I can't believe I hadn't seen it before.

And thanks to labels like Vinegar Syndrome, Severin, and Radiance, we've got a new wave of curators doing the work—restoring lost films and presenting them with care. Blind-buying their releases brings back the same feeling I had in video stores: picking something weird, not knowing what to expect, hoping for the best. I would've never witnessed the insanity that is *Boardinghouse* if I hadn't looked at the cover, thought "What the fuck is this?" and added it to my cart. Now John Wintergate's bizarre, shot-on-video vision is permanently burned into my brain.

But that feeling—that deeper connection with what we consume—is becoming rare. Today, most people encounter films by scrolling, skimming, and settling. The algorithm suggests something, and more often than not, we're like, "Okay, sure," knowing that if it doesn't grab us, we can just try something else. In that shift, something vital has been lost.

And I say this as someone who has made a show for Netflix and a film for Amazon. (And I hope to do so again—the audience reach is staggering.) But I do wonder: have some of my own films quietly disappeared into the endless scroll? And when people do watch, are they engaging with the same curiosity or intentionality as if they'd discovered the work on their own?

In the middle of this noisy, metric-driven culture we now live in, Jeff Rauseo's voice stands out: calm, sincere, steady. Watching him talk about a Criterion release or a boutique Blu-ray feels like being back in the video store, talking to the one clerk who's truly, infectiously passionate about movies. I put on his YouTube videos while I do the dishes—because as I'm struggling and hustling to get my next project made, it's a reminder that there's still an audience out there whose love for the art form comes from such a pure place.

That's why he's the perfect person to write this book.

Lost in the Stream isn't a takedown of streaming. It's a thoughtful interrogation of where we are, how we got here, and where we're headed. What do we lose when we stop choosing what we watch? What does it mean when curiosity gives way to convenience? What happens when filmmaking starts bending to metrics—when creative decisions are not guided by instinct, but by data? And what happens when people think of it as content, instead of what it is: art?

This book is a quiet reminder that the spark you felt at five years old—sitting in the dark, heart racing, completely transported—can still be lit. And that if we protect it, that feeling doesn't just fade. It becomes something we carry with us.

—*Michael Mohan*

INTRODUCTION

I know this sounds super cliche, but movies have truly been a part of my life for as long as I can remember. I have distinct memories from each "phase" of my life that tie back to specific events and people, but there is a constant across each phase of life: movies were a part of it in one way or another.

Some of my first memories are from trips to Disney World and MGM Studios (for my money, the best park at Disney), or Universal Studios in Orlando, Florida, exploring the magic of movies and falling in love with favorites like *Star Wars*, *Indiana Jones*, *E.T.*, and *King Kong* all over again.

Growing up on the East Coast, this was the closest that I was going to get to Hollywood without a cross-country trip, and it blew me away every time we went. Fortunately, we had a place to stay, as my dad's parents had a small home in a retirement community near the parks. This meant we got to go at least once a year for the first several years of my life, which was incredible.

I also fondly remember many summer weeks spent on Cape Cod at my grandparents' house in Eastham, Massachusetts. Those long summer days were full of outdoor activities, enjoying the beautiful National Seashore beaches, going for long bike rides on the rail trail, competing fiercely with a round of mini golf at Cape

Escape, and swimming at Great Pond. But the rainy days held an equally special place in my heart.

Rainy days meant we would be mixing a movie into a day filled with other activities like Scrabble, a game of poker, or an all-nighter of Star Wars: Monopoly with my uncle Doug—a fellow movie fanatic who was also a huge influence in that part of my life. I know my parents were very appreciative of the countless hours he spent with us on those Monopoly marathons after long weeks on vacation.

In between the inevitable chaos of my two brothers and me trying to be civil during our games, we always found time for a good movie. It could be something from the small selection of VHS tapes we had at the house (including *Jaws* and the original 1933 *King Kong*). Or, it could be a showing at the local theater, Wellfleet Cinemas, which is still around today and features one of the last remaining drive-in theaters in the US.

My memories also go back to throwing on *Jurassic Park* or *Small Soldiers* for the hundredth time in the VCR/TV combination in my parents' conversion van as we made our way back from a day at my grandparents' lake house in New Hampshire. The ride from the lake back to our house was almost exactly ninety minutes, which made it perfect for watching a movie. So, that's what we did almost every time.

I was born in 1992, so for most of my younger childhood, plenty of video stores were still around. We had a Blockbuster down the road from my house that I frequented, both for movies and video games. Browsing those shelves and walking around the store built a personal library of movies I wanted to check out, even if I wasn't old enough to watch them yet. I remember the terrifying cover art for movies like *Evil Dead II*, *Jack Frost*, and *The Texas Chainsaw Massacre*, and the promotional materials for things like *Saving Private Ryan*, *The Matrix*, and *Austin Powers*. I knew I wanted to see those movies based on the artwork and marketing alone, and I still get transported back to those days when I see them in my personal collection today.

Since the statute of limitations has probably passed (and since everyone my age would probably all be fined together for this), I should also mention how big a deal it was to have a VCR recorder in the 1990s. You could turn on HBO, pop in a tape, hit record, and have a copy of your favorite movie. Even with all of the legitimate VHS tapes we had in the house, we might have had even more recordings. Some were from friends and family and some were our doing, but it was just another key piece of technology and a unique experience that kids today won't understand.

As I hit my teenage years and my interests changed, movies were still a big part of my life, whether intentionally or not. One of the major things was getting introduced to horror movies through my mother. I had no idea that she was a fan as a child, but as I got older and into middle school, she started to share some of her favorites with me. *Halloween* stood out the most, and it keyed in on my obsession with the holiday. Fun fact: I was supposed to be born on Halloween. That was my due date, but I held out for ten days longer. It was almost meant to be, but I always had that in the back of my mind as something that connected me with the spooky season.

Every October, I would get home from school, throw down my backpack, ignore whatever homework I had (sorry to my teachers who might be reading this), and turn the TV right to AMC for their annual FearFest. I watched *Halloween* and all of the sequels, *Leprechaun* and its sequels, *Friday the 13th*, *Carrie*, and many more classics that AMC had on repeat all month.

I was mature for my age, so I think that made it "okay" in my mom's eyes, but these were also TV edits, so the amount of violence and sexual content was as low as cable TV would allow for, meaning not much. I liked the

Halloween sequels with Danielle Harris the most. They were faster-paced and featured more Michael Myers, so that was a plus for my teenage brain with a limited attention span.

I also vividly remember going to the movie theater every Friday night after freshman basketball games during the winter of 2007–2008. I saw a ton of movies that year, both good and bad, because we went as a team and saw whatever was available and new from the week before.

Being only fourteen, we weren't getting into the R-rated stuff, so it was a lot of PG-13 comedies, action movies, and horror movies. One of the most memorable movies was a remake of a Japanese horror film called *One Missed Call*. The original Japanese film is fairly well-known overseas and spawned a trilogy of sequels, so much like *The Ring* and *The Grudge*, American studios thought they might have another hit on their hands with an English remake of *One Missed Call*. However, the reason it was so memorable was because of how completely bonkers that movie was! I have not seen it in many years, but I think I am due for a rewatch because I remember it having some Syfy Channel-esque CGI effects and absurdity that had my whole team laughing. I vividly remember seeing other films like *The Strangers* (we had parental assistance for that one due to its rating), *Disturbia*, *Never Back Down*, and

Step Up 3. Yeah, they weren't the cream of the crop, but they have all stuck with me over the years as part of the formative movies I watched growing up. Good or bad, it was always fun to see what was out there each week and have something to talk about the next week at practice.

As high school progressed, I continued to watch a ton of movies. My dad was big into collecting DVDs when that format was released in the late '90s, so we had a decent collection of his favorites. We were also early subscribers to Netflix when they mailed DVDs to customers. We would get up to three discs at a time, and I had some say over where things stood in the queue. I saw a lot of great movies through that service, including the first movie that truly scared me, *The Ring*. I watched that with my mom, because, as my dad will still tell you to this day, "The DVD menu scared me so much I immediately shut it off." Needless to say, Dad was not a fan of horror movies.

At the time, I didn't have a DVD player, but I had an Xbox and a PlayStation, so I jumped right into his collection. I watched *Training Day* for the first time in my room and my mind was blown by how amazing Denzel Washington was, and how kick-ass an R-rated movie could be. I also found some of my favorite thrillers, including a hidden gem called *Arlington Road*, and one of David Fincher's best and unfortunately most often forgotten films, *The Game*. And, of course, we had the "dad movie" classics like *Back to the Future*, *Indiana Jones*, *Die Hard*, and *Terminator 2*. I would guess that we had around a hundred discs, mostly action and adventure movies. But I ran through that collection like my personal video store until I was old enough to start building my own.

When I got to college in the fall of 2011, streaming was starting to grow in popularity. Netflix had its service, and HBO, Hulu, and Amazon launched theirs in the same year. Compared to the world of today, where Netflix is primarily original content with each major Hollywood studio having a proprietary service, 2011's Netflix was a gold mine for college kids. I watched many movies for the first time that year in friends' dorm rooms and on my own setup: a thirty-two-inch TV with an Xbox 360. For 2011, I was living large.

One of the most memorable films I discovered in college was *The Big Lebowski*, which some friends and I stumbled upon one night looking for something to watch. I can honestly say I had never seen anything like it before. It was quirky, funny, unique, and had amazing writing and performances. That night made me think about the movies I was missing and opened my eyes to more independent films that might not be bestsellers but deserve to be seen.

The Big Lebowski is another example of a film that the algorithms of modern streaming services might have lost forever. *The Big Lebowski* gained its cult following through video rentals and word of mouth, and by 2011 it was popular enough to be featured on Netflix. However, if it had been released in 2023, would it have built the same cult following? Would it become one of the most quotable movies of all time? I honestly don't think so. And I say that understanding the irony that I would not have discovered it myself without the 2011 version of Netflix's algorithm. But things have changed, and movies have begun to be treated as "content," which is far more disposable.

The rest of my collegiate experience is one of the major catalysts that kick started my deep dive into the world of movies throughout my twenties. I majored in political science, but I took interesting classes like "Sports and Politics" and "Politics in Film" where I saw documentaries like *Hoop Dreams* about inner-city basketball prospects with their eyes set on the NBA, and *When We Were Kings* about the great Muhammad Ali and George Foreman "Rumble in the Jungle." I saw political thrillers like *The Manchurian Candidate* (the original—as much as I love

Denzel, the remake is meh), *All the President's Men*, and *The Ides of March*. I was watching tons of movies across new genres and decades and going back to my house at night and watching more.

The freedom of college also meant that I probably saw more movies in theaters from 2011–2014 than I ever will again and ever had before. I could see a movie every Tuesday night and get two tickets for me and my girlfriend (now wife) for twelve dollars. We saw things that I liked and things that she liked and mixed in a ton of different new release movies over those years. We also attended our first film festival together with my aforementioned uncle Doug and my aunt Donna, Independent Film Festival Boston, where I was exposed to another new subculture of independent film, documentaries, shorts, and a real sense of community that loved movies.

I became obsessed. I wanted to see everything, and as all the video stores closed around me, I wanted to start my own collection to enjoy and access in the highest quality. So, I took the little money that I earned working summer camps and odd jobs throughout college and made what ended up becoming one of the best investments in my life.

With only a couple thousand dollars in my bank account, I wanted to upgrade my movie-watching experience with a cheap surround sound system and a new TV. I found a cheap all-in-one Samsung surround sound system for $300 and a nice forty-inch HDTV for another $400. For $700, I had turned my childhood bedroom into a movie theater, and I could not have been happier.

One of the first things I noticed was that instead of a typical audio/video receiver, this system used a Blu-ray player to power the speakers. At the time, I knew next to nothing about Blu-ray versus DVD, audio tracks, surround sound, or anything that would have helped me figure out why my dad's DVDs didn't look as clear as my video games or Netflix streaming app. The internet said that if I got my hands on some Blu-rays instead of DVDs that I would upgrade both my audio and visual experience. Netflix wasn't offering those discs through the mail at this point, so I hopped in the car and went to Walmart, where I bought my first Blu-ray: *Training Day*. I put the disc in that night, and my life changed forever.

Pretty soon, the collection grew beyond just Denzel movies. I had to go get my favorites like *Jaws*, *Star Wars*, *Jurassic Park*, *Back to the Future*, and many more. Birthdays and Christmases were full of new movies, pulled from an updated list I maintained as I tried to find the best deals and the best movies to fill out my collection. Before I knew it, I had a closet full of movies. Then another bookshelf was full. Then an additional bookshelf and some floating shelves went up around the room. There were hundreds of them, and I was well on my way to becoming the collector and hardcore movie enthusiast that I am now.

From there, the rest is public history that has been cataloged across social media. I started a YouTube channel in late 2017 called "Films at Home," talking about my collection, physical media, and various home theater topics. I grew that over the years into a channel with over 100,000 subscribers, paired with a large social media following on other apps like TikTok and Instagram. As of the time of writing this introduction, I now have nearly a million followers across social media under my new handle @jeffrauseo, which may be how you found out about this book. I have expanded my content beyond physical media and my movie collection to talk about movies I love, give movie recommendations, and help people "find movies outside the algorithm."

After a couple more moves, in 2022, I settled in southern New Hampshire with my wife and two kids in a beautiful house in a quiet neighborhood. Well, mostly quiet, unless I am playing a movie too loudly. I have an awesome office space where I still work a nine-to-five job (thankfully remote!) and am surrounded by my favorite movies, memorabilia, and mementos. At this point, my current movie collection sits somewhere between 3,000–3,500 discs, all either HD Blu-ray or the new 4K UHD Blu-ray format.

Other than my family, this is my pride and joy. This is what I have wanted since I was a kid, looking at those shelves in the video store and dreaming of a house with a big screen to watch my movies. I know that five-year-old kid watching *Jaws* would be proud right now.

So, that's me. That is what got me to where I am today, which all led to me writing this book and sharing my passion for film online with hundreds of thousands of other similarly-minded followers. But other than getting to know me better, there is a reason I got so detailed in my history and how it relates to movies.

As you saw, each little experience I had contributed to the movies I love today as an adult. A lot of what I wrote about probably sounded familiar or struck a nostalgic nerve with people my age. Every experience that led me to find movies that I love and cherish today was real and human. If it was a shared experience, like watching movies with friends in our dorm rooms, that was an in-person interaction with people I knew. The video stores carried physical copies of movies, as did the big-box retailers where I started my collection. It was all real, authentic, and human.

If you grew up in the '80s and '90s, you understand what I'm saying. The world was different. There were less distractions. You found movies through friends and family or through books like this. There were no algorithms that followed your every move, pushing constant distractions in front of you wherever they could reach you. Texts, emails, phone calls, social media, streaming apps—the content is endless. We are presented with so many choices, yet at the same time limited, with less "freedom" than we've ever had as humans to find something unique that speaks to us.

I understand the irony of someone who has built a large social media following saying that the internet and algorithms have had a negative effect on the film industry. But I would argue that this is also a major reason why I started doing what I do online. I did not find communities that thought like I did. Plenty of people were talking about movies, most often the latest and greatest Hollywood blockbusters that would please the algorithm and get the clicks. And if they enjoy doing that, all the power to them.

I love a big Hollywood blockbuster as much as the next guy, and I watch their content when it interests me. But I wanted more. I wanted to find movies in a more traditional way, through community and shared experiences. And in today's world, the best way to do that and reach "my people" is to get online and start posting. I know I am adding to the noise, but I hope that my noise is gentler, different, and more appealing than some of what is out there right now in the world of movie discussion.

As an extension of that philosophy, I have written the book you are holding in your hands, reading on your Kindle, or listening to while you do the dishes. See— technology is great sometimes. Trust me, I am not a Luddite. You should see all the tech in my house. All I want is a balance, and as it relates to movies, a refocus on human connection and experiences versus the current focus on what will get the most clicks and please the algorithms and the shareholders.

In this book, I want to explore the changes in how we have consumed and connected with movies over time. How did our habits change from the days of the drive-in and small local theaters to the world of massive Cineplex chains and eighty-five-inch TVs in our living rooms? How did the experience of choosing what to watch change as we introduced home video, video rental stores, streaming services, and premium cable TV shows that rival the production value of a feature film? How did the types of movies that get made change based on algorithms and analytics?

I think everyone can take something away from this analysis of the current state of film and have good discussions that start to change how we think about what I believe is the most important art form we have as humans. So, thank you for getting this far, thank you for purchasing this book and supporting me, and now, let's dive in!

PART 1

A BRIEF HISTORY OF MOVIES & HOW WE WATCHED THEM

Over the last hundred years, society and technology have moved at an incredible pace. We went from the Wright Brothers' first flight in 1903 to putting a man on the moon in 1969. Now, the phones in our pockets are 100,000 times faster than the computers that put those men on the moon. The advancement of human civilization is amazing, sometimes terrifying, and inevitable. The technology that drives the film industry and the delivery systems used to deliver movies to consumers is no stranger to change either. However, for decades, the delivery systems were largely the same, even as the technology behind the making of the movies advanced.

From the time that the first modern movie theaters opened in the 1920s and 1930s up until the 1950s, audiences had one option for visual entertainment: going to the movies. In the days before television, movies were an event, like a concert or a play, and people would get dressed up, line up for tickets, and enjoy the buzz in the crowd. Although it may seem like movie theaters have taken a turn for the worse since the COVID-19 pandemic and the explosion of at-home entertainment options and streaming services, that is not the case. Movie theater ticket sales have been on the decline since television went mainstream in the late 1950s, and the market for theatrical movies has been constantly adapting and shrinking since the years following World War II.

The 1940s, and 1946, in particular, were the peak years for American cinema in terms of tickets sold. In 1946, American movie theaters sold over four billion tickets, equal to thirty tickets per capita based on the population of the United States at the time.[2] In times of distress, people have always looked for an escape, and movies are one of the best escapes we have. Based on the timing, it was a perfect storm: the Hollywood system ramped up both production numbers and quality in the late 1930s and 1940s, and the American public was desperately looking for a distraction from all of the horrible news coming from abroad.

On top of that, the US government was pulling in celebrated filmmakers to create propaganda films during the war. The most famous of the bunch were Frank Capra, John Ford, John Huston, George Stevens, and William Wyler. These five directors were the focus of Mark Harris's book and subsequent documentary, *Five Came Back*, which is a must-read and must-see material for fans of history and film. During this unique time in film history, the American public went to the movies to get the latest updates on the war. These films surely resulted in millions of additional tickets being sold

2   Michelle C. Pautz, "The Decline in Average Weekly Cinema Attendance, 1930–2000," University of Dayton Political Science Faculty Publications, 2002, ecommons.udayton.edu/pol_fac_pub/25.

to a public desperate for more information in the age before television.

After the war, movie ticket sales declined dramatically because of the competition that came with television's rise in popularity. In 1950, it is estimated that around 8 percent of US households had a television. By 1955, that number increased to 50 percent, and by 1960, it was at 90 percent.[3] This rapid rise meant that more people were staying home and enjoying their TV at home. It was new, it was exciting, and it brought entertainment into the home in a way that hadn't been seen since the earliest days of radio.

As more people stayed home, ticket sales dipped hard. By the mid-1950s, ticket sales had dropped from their all-time high of over four billion down to less than 2.5 billion. By the mid-1960s, they had dropped to around one billion.[4] People's habits were shifting, and although movies continued to make lots of money, it was due to the increased ticket prices, not increased sales. Around this same time, the line between TV and movies began to blur

3   Michelle C. Pautz, "The Decline in Average Weekly Cinema Attendance, 1930–2000," University of Dayton Political Science Faculty Publications, 2002, ecommons.udayton.edu/pol_fac_pub/25.

4   Michelle C. Pautz, "The Decline in Average Weekly Cinema Attendance, 1930–2000," University of Dayton Political Science Faculty Publications, 2002, ecommons.udayton.edu/pol_fac_pub/25.

for the first time as films began showing on network TV stations and "made for TV" movies became more popular.

Up until the 1960s, TV networks that wanted to broadcast films were relegated to using lower-tier projects, as most Hollywood productions were being protected by the studios to safeguard them against losing viewership to the television revolution. As the 1960s rolled around, Hollywood came around (or was forced to adapt) to the idea of showing films on TV, and NBC launched the first network TV movie program called "NBC Saturday Night at the Movies," which ran from 1961 to 1978. NBC's program was the first to focus on larger, more recent theatrical releases and was the first mainstream option for audiences to watch movies at home without needing to go to the theater. CBS and ABC followed suit with their own programs, turning the once-a-week movie into a competitive landscape that would draw in millions of viewers.

When *Gone with the Wind* aired on NBC over two nights in 1976, it received a Nielsen rating of 47.7, meaning almost 48 percent of the televisions in America were tuned in to the movie those nights. To put that into perspective, that is a larger share than all but four Super Bowls.[5] This new

---

5   Peter Krämer, *The New Hollywood: From Bonnie and Clyde to Star Wars* (Wallflower Press, 2005), 46.

era also ushered in hundreds of "made for TV" movies, which became extremely popular in the 1970s and 1980s. Films like *The Day After*, a grim depiction of a fictional nuclear conflict between the United States and USSR, premiered on ABC in 1983 with a 46 rating (46 percent of all households were tuned in) and over 100 million viewers.[6] Older movies also got a second life through network broadcasts, being shown to audiences for the first time in decades after their initial theatrical runs. The network broadcasts of movies like *The Wizard of Oz* and *It's a Wonderful Life* created a massive spike in popularity for these films that had otherwise been largely forgotten. TV was the new revolution in entertainment, and the public was locked in.

TV broadcasts had their limitations, though. The FCC (Federal Communications Commission) has always cracked down on what could be shown on network TV, meaning most R-rated films required significant cuts that resulted in "network cuts" for popular films that, in some cases, drastically changed the impact of the film. Imagine trying to watch *The Exorcist* on network TV. CBS aired it in 1980, but the cuts changed the film and did not

6   Brian Lowry, "*Seinfeld*'s Finale Ends up in Sixth Place of All Time," *Los Angeles Times*, May 16, 1998, latimes.com/archives/la-xpm-1998-may-16-ca-50143-story.html.

create an ideal experience for audiences based on the censorship required.[7]

Another player on the scene in the early 1970s was HBO and the advent of the premium cable subscription. HBO launched in 1972 and offered premium, ad-free programming of movies, sports, and other entertainment for a monthly fee. Although it had a slow start, HBO was available in most major cities by the late 1970s, reaching over one million subscribers by the end of 1977.[8] Customers could enjoy movies ad-free and uninterrupted as HBO profited from the subscription fees instead of advertisers. For this same reason, audiences could enjoy their films censorship-free without the stringent requirements of the FCC wearing down on them or advertisers who wouldn't be comfortable with their products next to some more controversial topics.

Right around the same time that HBO found its footing and premium cable competitors like Showtime hit the market, the movie industry was about to go through yet another revolution as VHS, Betamax, and home video made their long-awaited arrival. VHS and Betamax were first launched in 1975 and 1976, respectively, followed

---

7   *"The Exorcist,"* Movie-Censorship.com, August 23, 2021, movie-censorship.com/report.php?ID=136647.

8   "Cable Brief: Million Mark," Broadcasting Publications, Inc., December 26, 1976, worldradiohistory.com/Archive-BC/BC-1976/1976-12-27-BC.pdf.

by Laserdisc in 1978. Movies were now available to watch at home at the viewer's convenience, with pause, fast forward, and rewind options to control the movie experience. The first few years of these new home video formats were expensive, as many releases were priced for rental stores that would make recurring revenue from each movie. Selling VHS tapes for $99 or more was common, but as consumers adopted the new formats and the equipment became more widely available and less expensive, eventually the prices dropped. For around $20 to $30, movie lovers could own their favorite films, build a collection, and watch their tapes over and over again for a single cost.

Meanwhile, movie theaters had hit their first rock bottom in the early 1970s when ticket sales dipped below one billion for the first time in decades.[9] Television and home video had made their mark, and theaters were permanently changed as a result. From the 1970s until the early 2000s, ticket sales remained fairly stable, hovering between 1–1.5 billion until they "peaked" again in 2002 when sales cracked that 1.5 billion ticket ceiling with 1.6 billion tickets sold.[10] However, that would be the last time the industry would hit that high, as

9   Alexander L. Taylor III, "Bad Days at the Box Office," *TIME*, June 1, 1981, time.com/archive/6700486/bad-days-at-the-box-office.

10   "Domestic Movie Theatrical Market Summary 1995 to 2025," The Numbers, the-numbers.com/market.

through the rest of the 2000s and into the 2010s, ticket sales slowly dipped from 1.5 billion down to 1.2 billion in 2019.[11] Then, another perfect storm hit in the form of a global pandemic and a huge uptick in streaming services that offered a revolution in entertainment not seen since the earliest days of television.

As COVID-19 reared its ugly head in 2020 and forced all movie theaters worldwide to close their doors, the major studios needed to find a way to keep their doors open. Without theaters, they had lost their biggest revenue stream, so they looked for what might work instead. They didn't have to look far. The internet had matured, most people had high-speed connections, and the success of services like Netflix, Hulu, and Amazon Prime made the decision easy—they needed their own streaming services.

In some weird stroke of luck or foresight, Disney launched their service first in November 2019, just before the first cases of COVID-19 were announced in December of that year. Warner Brothers had a service already (HBO Go), but it was relegated to just the HBO properties. In May 2020, they launched a new service when they announced HBO Max, now known simply as

---

11   "Domestic Movie Theatrical Market Summary 1995 to 2025," The Numbers, the-numbers.com/market.

Max after a full Warner-Discovery merger. In July 2020, Universal quickly followed suit by launching Peacock. Finally, Paramount launched its service, Paramount+, in March 2021. In just one year since the world shut down in March 2020, audiences went from having virtually no studio-owned streaming services to having each of the four biggest studios with their own platforms. It was a complete whirlwind that in retrospect does not feel like it happened as quickly as it did, but in those dark days of COVID-19 lockdowns, everything felt slower.

Sony/Columbia is still the only studio of the "Big Five"—Warner Brothers, Universal, Disney, Sony, and Paramount—not to invest in a new service, instead licensing their titles and making money that way instead of standing up a costly software launch. I could go on and on about the pros and cons of each and why so many studios seem to be struggling financially (hint—it could be the huge losses associated with launching a global software platform when you are just an entertainment company) but maybe that's for another book. Either way, even without Sony's platform, the world had changed forever.

One of the biggest shifts that spelled doom for movie theaters and changed the way we watched movies forever was when the studios started releasing first-run, would-be theatrical releases straight to their services. This was a massive break from the decades-long agreements between movie theaters and the studios where the theatrical window would often be around ninety days. These were exclusive agreements that would have resulted in massive lawsuits and fighting if they were broken, and they were the law of the land when it came to movie theaters and their relationships with the studios.

With COVID-19 forcing the theaters to remain closed for months and then at partial capacity for months longer, the studios had an excuse to break this agreement and start experimenting with shorter or nonexistent theatrical windows. Major films like *Wonder Woman 1984* and Disney/Pixar's *Soul* went right to Max and Disney+, skipping theatrical runs and going out to subscribers for free. Other films like *Mulan* were offered to subscribers on Disney+ for a $30 fee in addition to limited theatrical runs. Peacock and Universal released many movies at home on the same day as theaters, like *Halloween Kills*, one that I was happy about as a huge *Halloween* fan who had a newborn and six-week-postpartum wife I was not about to risk taking to a theater.

Side note—I liked *Halloween Kills* a lot and I will defend that to my end days as one of the purest slasher films ever made. It was like something straight out of the 1980s and the heyday of the genre. Of course it is a little goofy and cheesy, as most of your favorite slashers are, but this was awesome because it was Michael Myers at his peak power. It was like watching Darth Vader at the end of *Rogue One*, but for an entire movie. If you love Michael Myers, you should love *Halloween Kills*. Rant over.

With all of the shifts being made to the theatrical windows and movie theaters losing all of their bargaining chips, the post-COVID-19 world of movies looks strikingly similar to the world we experienced during the pandemic. As a collector of physical media, it is amazing to me how quickly new movies hit the Blu-ray and 4K UHD formats. There are often preorders up on the same day the movie hits theaters. For example, *Nosferatu* released in theaters on December 25, 2024, and came to Blu-ray on February 18, 2025. For those of us who grew up waiting six months or more for movies to come to VHS and DVD, it is crazy to see how quick the turnaround is now.

In the digital world, it is even quicker. If a movie bombs, you can expect to see it available for digital rental in about two to three weeks. Even if it is a massive success, like 2024's *Wicked*, you can expect it to be available for home viewing in about five to six weeks. *Wicked* hit theaters on November 22, 2024, and by December 31, 2024, it was available to watch at home. That is unheard of for a movie that made over $400 million domestically and $700 million worldwide.[12]

On top of all of those headwinds, movies also had new entertainment options to contend with as the rise of social media video platforms took over the public consciousness. The average person now spends fifty-three minutes per day on TikTok,[13] forty-eight minutes per day on YouTube,[14] and thirty-three minutes per day on Instagram.[15] Of course, some of that mindless scrolling is done during a slow time at work, waiting for your friends at a restaurant, or my favorite, on the good old ceramic throne. But if you look at how many minutes per day the average person spends on social media, it adds up. Just between the three big apps—TikTok, YouTube, and Instagram—users spend over two hours scrolling each day. That's a feature-length

12   *"Wicked,"* Box Office Mojo, boxofficemojo.com/release/rl1199474177.

13   "TikTok Users: Statistics and Trends for 2025," Backlinko, last modified April 2025, backlinko.com/tiktok-users.

14   "Average Time Spent on YouTube (2019–2024)," Oberlo, last modified January 2024, oberlo.com/statistics/average-time-spent-on-youtube.

15   "Average Time Spent per Day by US Adult Users on Select Social Media Platforms, 2023," EMARKETER, June 1, 2023, emarketer.com/chart/263759/average-time-spent-per-day-by-us-adult-users-on-select-social-media-platforms-2023-minutes.

movie's worth of time spent on social media. When you add in all of the options available on cable TV and streaming services for shorter-form sitcoms or reality shows, you can see why movie theaters, and movies in general, are struggling.

When a movie was released in 1946, theaters and studios had to compete with radio programs and other live shows for entertainment. Now, they are competing with themselves and their own streaming apps and shows, social media, television, and live entertainment and concerts. There are more options than ever for entertainment, and much of it is designed to capture the short attention spans of the current generations of humans. Movies have tried to adapt to this shift—in many ways, to their detriment.

Sticking with the theme of how our movie-watching habits have shifted over the last couple of decades as consumers, I thought it would be fun to take you on a time-travel trip to a simpler time for movie lovers. A time before streaming apps and algorithms. It may seem like a long time ago, but it wasn't. Most of you reading this book were alive during this time and probably remember it fondly. I know I do.

Consider me your "Ghost of Movie Nights Past" as we jump back to the year 2000 and follow a fictional thirty-year-old movie lover who wants to have an at-home movie date night with their partner. Then we will leave the year 2000 and jump ahead to 2025, where another thirty-year-old film fan is looking to do the same. It may not feel like the time jump is that crazy, but the differences in the experience are going to be quite the revelation when it is all laid out in front of you. Let me paint this picture for you and let those vivid memories of a simpler time come rushing back.

It's 5:30 p.m. on a cool Friday night in the fall of 2000. You are just getting home from work and decided that tonight would be a great night for some pizza and a movie at home. You get in the house and run it by your partner who wholeheartedly agrees that a movie sounds great. There isn't anything good on TV tonight anyway and you don't feel like getting dressed up to go out to the theater.

You head over to your small shelf of DVDs and VHS tapes, looking for something to watch for the night, but nothing jumps out at you. You own most of your favorite movies, but you are looking for something new and exciting. You glance over at the fridge to check the hours of your local video store on the magnet you grabbed during your last visit. Luckily, it's a Friday, so they are open late. That will give you plenty of time to browse the shelves and find something perfect.

You hop in your car and head on down to the local rental store. There is a Blockbuster down the road as well, but you prefer supporting local businesses. You have had a longtime connection with the owners of the local store, and with Blockbusters popping up everywhere, you feel lucky that you still have that relationship. Plus, they have a much better selection of independent films and hard-to-find stuff that mainstream stores like Blockbuster or Hollywood Video don't carry.

When you get to the store, you are immediately greeted by the clerk at the front desk. They all know you well in the store, and you have had many conversations with the owners and staff about films you enjoy. You and the staff have shared dozens of reviews and recommendations back and forth. They know what you like, and they are always happy to find something new and unique, which is perfect, because that's what you are looking for tonight.

As you say hello to the clerk and have some small talk, you mention recently having seen *Don't Look Now*, an amazing film from 1973 directed by Nicolas Roeg and starring Donald Sutherland and Julie Christie. You enjoyed the sense of dread and terror that played with your emotions throughout the film and you loved the wild ending that had you thinking about it for days afterward. That type of thriller has been right in your wheelhouse lately, and you'd love to find more like it.

The clerk at this store knows their way around a movie recommendation and immediately thinks of films in a similar style. You both head over to the psychological thriller section and browse together. You come across a few movies you have seen before that would fit the bill, like *Rosemary's Baby*, *Dressed to Kill*, and *The Changeling*. As much as you love them, you want something new. So, you keep looking, picking up titles off the shelf and holding them in your hand while you read the cover notes and take in the artwork.

Finally, you find it. *Sisters*, a film from 1972 by director Brian De Palma. You've been enjoying the vibe of movies from this time, and you are a big fan of De Palma's other work. You haven't heard of *Sisters*, but based on the DVD cover art and description, it looks promising. You show it to the clerk, who recognizes it, and they give you their short review. You both agree it is a good pick and head over to the counter to check out. At the counter, you grab a couple of candy packs and a small pamphlet highlighting new releases for this month, and you sign out *Sisters* for a three-day rental. You hand over the cash, scan your membership card to earn another entry toward a free rental, thank the clerk for the help, and head on your way.

After stopping at the local pizza place to pick up your order, you get home and start to settle in for the night. Your partner gets the plates out and starts making some drinks while you sit down and fire up the DVD player. You open the case, take out the disc, and pop it in the player. Then you sit down and enjoy two hours of uninterrupted bliss in your living room, mesmerized by the craziness of Brian De Palma and *Sisters*.

I remember days like this well. I wasn't an adult in 2000 (I was eight), but I loved going to the video store and grabbing some food on the way home. We might have picked out a movie or a game or a new show—I watched many episodes of *Batman: The Animated Series* and *Teenage Mutant Ninja Turtles* on rented VHS tapes— but the trip itself was an adventure. Then you got home and jumped into another adventure. It all felt special and magical in a way.

Now, let's jump to 2025. It is the same scenario—you want to grab some pizza and have a Friday night movie at home with your partner. But things have changed...

It's 5:00 p.m., and you've just logged off for the weekend. It's 2025, so you and your partner both work from home on Fridays. You are both wiped out from last weekend and a long week of work, so you decide that getting takeout and watching something at home would beat going out to eat and heading to the theater.

The first thing you want to do is order your food, and your phone is already pinging you with offers from different food delivery apps. They know you like to order dinner on Fridays, so the coupons start rolling in before you even open the app. You settle on one of the big pizza chains because they seem to have the best deal. You prefer the local place, but they don't deliver through the apps, and you don't feel like making a call or going to pick it up.

While you wait for your food to arrive, you and your partner sit on the couch and turn on the TV. You haven't owned DVDs or Blu-rays in years, and at this point, you don't even have a player that could use them anyway. You start browsing through the different apps—Prime Video, Netflix, Hulu, Max, Paramount+, Apple TV+—and try to think of what's available on each of them. You have been on a comedy kick lately, so it would be cool to find something funny and new to watch for the first time. Earlier in the day, you saw a video on Instagram where someone (@JeffRauseo, of course—shameless plug) had recommended some underrated comedies. You and your partner like watching *Saturday Night Live* and are big fans of Andy Samberg and The Lonely Island, so you were intrigued by *Hot Rod*, a smaller comedy from 2007 that featured some of your favorite actors.

You search for *Hot Rod* on your TV to see if it is on any of the services you subscribe to, but unfortunately, it is not. You could rent it from Amazon for $4, but that seems silly when you are already paying upward of $50 a month for access to your streaming apps. So, you forget that and open Netflix to see if anything stands out. There are a few new comedy series with big names attached to them, but you don't want to start a new show. You want a movie, something that you can start and finish tonight without needing to binge-watch all weekend.

You have been on a true crime kick lately, so your Netflix recommendations are flooded with true crime documentaries and series. After scrolling and not finding anything that looks promising, you close Netflix for now and jump over to Hulu. Hulu has more of the same, with a handful of stuff you have already seen and a bunch of Hulu originals that look interesting but aren't what you want right now. As you are scrolling through each row of recommendations, you get a notification from your group chat on Instagram. One of your friends shared a video they thought was funny, so you open it up and check it out. You start flipping through some other videos when your phone goes off again. This time, it's Uber Eats. The pizza is here at your front door, and you still haven't picked a movie. Frustrating for sure, but now you need to decide, and fast.

After grabbing the pizza, your partner goes to get some plates and drinks. You grab the remote and open Max. Maybe there will be something to watch on there? Luckily Max has a larger catalog of movies with all of the Warner Brothers catalog behind it. You just have to scroll through all of the reality TV shows and true crime series from their partnership with Discovery. Once you get there, you see a few familiar titles. *Legally Blonde* stands out amongst the crowd. It is something you have seen years before, but it's familiar and you know you like it. The pizza is here, and you are sick of scrolling mindlessly through apps. So, you check in with your partner to see if they are okay, then you click on the poster and head off to Harvard Law with Reese Witherspoon for the night.

As you are watching the movie, you get a few more texts from the group chat. One of them is from your best friend who says you "have to see this video," so you look down and check it out. It is a hilarious video, so you show your partner, who laughs out loud. They flip through to another video—it's a clip from an old episode of *It's Always Sunny in Philadelphia*, a show you both love. The clip reminds you that you still haven't finished the latest season, and you don't want to have anything spoiled for you the next time you hang out with your friends, who are also huge fans of the show. You are about forty-five minutes into *Legally Blonde*, but you've seen it before, and you are starting to lose interest. You both decide to switch it up, shut off the movie, and head back over to Hulu to watch *It's Always Sunny* and finish the latest season.

Is there anything inherently wrong with that scenario compared to the first one? No, not really. You still picked a movie that you enjoy, you got your pizza, and even though you changed your minds about the movie, you had a fun night. But the intentional decision making and the human connection were missing. Everything in that scenario was driven by algorithms, distractions, notifications, and information gathered about you and your interests by machine learning systems. From the pizza to the recommendations on the apps to the videos you saw on Instagram, everything was shown to you in order to get you to use their service.

The local pizza place never stood a chance when the big chain could send a $5 coupon and free delivery offers right to your phone, timed to hit at 5:15 p.m. as you get off work. Each app you opened was trying their best to show you what they thought you wanted to see, but they aren't human. They had no idea you were in the mood for a comedy. That goes against everything that you had taught them. Even when you did select a movie, quite passively, there were other entertainment options trying to distract you. You opened Instagram, watched a couple of videos, stumbled upon a clip from Hulu's Instagram page of *It's Always Sunny*, and that made you stop your movie and leave Max to go back to Hulu. Everything you touched was fighting for your attention, trying to get you to stay on their app or their service for as long as you could. They were all in constant competition to give your brain a dopamine hit and to hopefully give you another one before that one wears off.

Did you notice how much physical, social, and emotional connection there was in the first scenario? You physically drove to the store, taking that time to think about what you might want to watch. You spent time in the store talking to employees or other customers about what you have seen recently. You touched each DVD case or VHS box and picked up and put down several before you made a final choice. It is all intentional and slow. And it had to be! When you left the store, you weren't going to kill the rest of your night by driving back, returning the copy you picked, and then driving back home to try something new. You made a choice, and you were, for better or worse, stuck with it for the rest of the night.

There were also no distractions. There wasn't a device in your pocket that had unlimited information and entertainment, able to connect you to everyone in the world in seconds. Your entertainment options boiled down to what was showing on cable TV that night, the movies you had in your personal collection, and the one movie you picked from the rental store. You were locked in to the movie from start to finish, minus the occasional pause for a bathroom or snack break, and that meant you probably finished it. You had just paid $5 cash for the rental and you weren't about to let that go to waste. If you shut it off, that money might as well have been thrown away. And that did happen—sometimes the movies were bad. Sometimes you wouldn't like the movie. But you knew that the next time you went to the rental store, you could relay that information to the staff and discuss what you didn't like and what you might like instead.

All the streaming apps see when you shut off a movie is that you watched something for forty-five minutes. You may not have finished it, but that doesn't tell them you didn't like it. All it says is that they could capture your attention for forty-five minutes with a 2000s comedy starring Reese Witherspoon, so if they can find you similar movies or TV shows that fit that mold, they can get your attention once again, and maybe for longer next time. They want to make your decisions easy and comfortable. Taking a risk by making an outside-of-the-box recommendation means that they could be risking losing your attention and your trust to other applications. These streaming apps are as much about data collection and marketing as they are about entertainment. The longer you spend on the app, the more information they can get, and the more valuable their service becomes to advertisers. This is what drives the algorithm and revenue.

Clearly, a lot has changed in the last twenty-five years. Even more has changed in the last five years. The world of movies is changing so quickly that consumers and audiences can barely keep up. I feel the same struggle even as someone who might be more "in tune" than the average person. Ticket sales are down, prices are higher than ever, movie theaters are closing, algorithms run your daily life, and movies just don't feel the same as they used to.

So, how does it all work? What impact has this shift had on the way movies are made and consumed? How did COVID-19 accelerate this shift? Will movie theaters survive? And what can you do to break outside the algorithms and make informed decisions as a movie fan? The answers to all of these questions are complex, but by combining my knowledge and passion for marketing and film with deep research into these topics, I can certainly help you understand how these shifts are impacting you and what the future holds.

PART 2

THE ALGORITHMS
& THE STREAMING
REVOLUTION

How did you first hear about the last movie that you watched? It could have been from someone like me, sharing a video about a hidden gem or a new movie I was excited about. It could have been an article from *Variety* or *The Hollywood Reporter* shared on social media. It could have been from a paid advertisement that popped up when you opened Instagram, or a teaser playing ahead of the next YouTube video you planned to watch. Maybe you were on Reddit and scrolled through a popular thread on movies or saw someone who posted a new movie poster release. Chances are, no matter which way you found the movie, it was through an online source driven by algorithms.

It is the twenty-first century, after all, and we are all chronically online. That is how we get our information. Newspapers have become blogs, talk shows have become podcasts and YouTube channels, and commercials on cable TV have become paid partnerships with influencers on social media. For better or worse, the world is changing, and those of us who have lived over the last twenty to thirty years have been right in the middle of the biggest and fastest changes in technology and the dissemination of information that the world has ever seen.

However, the world of movies has changed even faster with the "Streaming Revolution," a shift that has brought more drastic changes to the entertainment industry than the previous hundred years that came before it. The Streaming Revolution was not brought on by the movie studios and production companies. It was brought on by technology companies, and as a result, our entertainment delivery systems shifted from a world of theaters and video tapes to a world of subscriptions, software, and algorithms.

Although we are all online and getting huge downloads of information every day, chances are that in the past few years your taste in movies and what you decide to watch has been affected more by machine learning and algorithms than any blogs or social media posts. And the scary part is, you may not even realize what this revolution is doing to you and your tastes, and how drastically it has changed the way you consume your favorite media.

Just like on social media, you are not in control of what gets put in front of you on a streaming service. When you open Netflix or Hulu, the titles that you see presented first are the ones that each service thinks you are most likely to watch based on your previous viewing habits. In many cases, these platforms also have additional data that they can use to push certain content, and you might be surprised at how much they know about you.

As someone who works in digital marketing for a living, I have been behind the scenes of many marketing platforms that collect data on just about everyone. With the current internet privacy laws in the United States and Canada, there are not many limitations to what can be collected. Once you click that annoying banner on every website that asks if it is okay to collect "cookies," you are being tracked.

I know not everyone fully understands how this all works, so let me break it down for you in layman's terms. To my fellow digital marketing friends out there, just bear with me for a moment. I know it is a lot more complicated than what I am about to say, but we aren't all digital marketing nerds.

For reference, cookies are small pieces of tracking code that are built into websites and allow them to see where you came from, how you got there, where you are located, and some other basic information based on your activities online.

If you have a Facebook account, a Gmail account, or any other social media platform, they all use cookies as well, and most modern websites have integrated that code into their own sites. For example, if you click an article from Facebook, and it brings you to *The New York Times*, Facebook knows what you clicked on and what you read.

Depending on your privacy settings, the *Times* may also know exactly who you are from the information that Facebook has collected and shared with the *Times*. This can vary depending on the website's privacy policies, but be honest, have you ever read one of those?

Europe has stricter laws, one of the most famous being GDPR (General Data Protection Regulation), so that data is more difficult to attain through website tracking tools like cookies. But even then, you would be surprised at how much information we all make publicly available on the internet. So, even you Europeans aren't safe from the claws of data collection if you're sharing personal information on public online forums.

Now you're probably asking how Facebook or Google knows all of that. They simply couldn't get that much information from just your website cookies! And you're right. They don't need the cookies, because of what we all freely share.

Think about your Facebook or Instagram account. What information can you gather from that? One of these services might find the email address that you signed up with, your marital or relationship status, maybe the high school or college that you attended, or a photo of you and your dog.

If they have your email, they can probably find you on LinkedIn. Now they know where you work and what you do for work. If your profile says that you're engaged to be married, they know that you might be looking for a wedding venue or a wedding ring in the future. That's valuable information for marketing teams who work for country clubs or jewelry stores. Don't be surprised to see ads for those things show up in your feed. They aren't "listening to your conversations." You gave that to them publicly.

Even if your profile is private, other people can share information about you inadvertently. If your mother tags you in a photo on Facebook that celebrates the birth of your first child, or the day you bought your first child home, they can see that. Now you're on an advertising list for diapers, even though you never publicly shared that you had a baby.

And outside of social media platforms, the same thing applies to your search and internet activity. If you visited a website looking for a new vacuum, or you went to a review website and read reviews on the best vacuums, you'd best believe that Dyson knows who you are. Don't be surprised if your next Hulu ad break features a commercial from Dyson. In fact, I would be surprised if it didn't.

If you are ever curious about just how much these companies know about you, you can request a download of your information. I guarantee you will be pretty shocked by what they know. I recently downloaded all of my data from my Google account in research for this book, and let me tell you, I think they knew more about me than anyone else, including myself. They knew things I forgot I ever did, like when I visited some obscure restaurant on a vacation a decade ago, or when I drove an old car that my father owned for a few months before trading it in for a new one. It was a ton of information that made me valuable to advertisers. It equated to over ten gigabytes of data, and an estimated six-figure, if not seven-figure, individual data points. If you are curious, search for "Google Takeout" and get your report so you can be as freaked out as I was.

I am online a lot and have more information out there than most with all of my content creation and public social media accounts, so I am probably a "white whale" in an advertiser's eyes. But even without that level of interaction, it is hard to believe what they capture about you, especially at the level that Google operates. Do you use Google Maps? They know everywhere you've traveled. Use Gmail? They know what is in your emails. Use Google Chrome and Google Search? They know everything. Hell, I am writing the first draft of this book in Google Docs, so they know about my writing before the people closest to me probably do!

So, why am I nerding out (and possibly scaring you) about the internet and all of the data that's out there? Because the streaming services have the same access to that data that the advertisers do, and they're sure to use it every time you fire up their app. They know where you live, your gender, your age, and tons of other information from other databases, and after a few weeks of using their service, they have a good idea of the types of entertainment that you enjoy.

I doubt anyone reads the privacy policies that these apps have, but if you do read them you can see that this is all hiding in plain sight. This isn't a big conspiracy, or "Big Brother" spying on you without your permission. We all give them permission by using their service. At the end of the day, streaming apps are not entertainment providers. That may be how they get your subscription: by providing exclusive, high-quality entertainment. But they are software companies with massive data centers that are providing a service and making as much money selling advertising on their platforms as they will with subscription fees. Even Netflix, the last holdout of the ad-free service for subscribers, has added an ad-supported tier. If you pay them enough, you can avoid the ads. If you want to save a few bucks and pay less, you are getting sold to advertisers. Either way, you are the product. That is just the reality of the modern world.

Going back to my opening question, let's think about it again. How did you first hear about the last movie you watched? As most of you likely said, it was through an online source. But it was also entirely out of your control. If you saw it from a social media post or a content creator like me, an algorithm pushed that content in front of you. If you saw a movie poster on Reddit, an algorithm pushed that to your front page. If you saw an article in your Google news alerts from *Variety* featuring an interview with Ben Affleck on his new movie, an algorithm made the decision to prompt you with that link.

This is what I and experts in this field of study would call "the illusion of choice." We have more choices than we have ever had to get our news, connect with our friends, listen to music, engage in our communities, and of course, watch movies and TV shows. But we aren't truly choosing any of that. It is all based on a machine that sucks up all of our data and spits it back out into tightly curated experiences that it believes we will enjoy.

While there are no definitive numbers on just how many algorithms we interact with each day, educated guesses by industry experts put that number around several hundred, if not 1,000 or more, every day. There are algorithms determining our healthcare, education, careers, criminal justice system, and of course, entertainment. If you are looking for a deeper dive into algorithms and the massive impact that they have in modern society, I highly recommend Hannah Fry's book *Hello World: Being Human in the Age of Algorithms*, which is a fascinating and occasionally terrifying look into this recent phenomenon.

These algorithms can also be difficult to break, or reset, which amplifies the echo chamber that users can get trapped in. There is a fascinating recent study out of the University of Pennsylvania and their Annenberg School for Communication's Computational Social Science Lab that aimed to determine how much impact YouTube algorithms versus user input played into the content that users would see on the platform.[16] The main goal of the study was to investigate the impact that YouTube's algorithm has on the radicalization of individuals. However, the most interesting part of that study for me was the experiment the team ran to determine how long it took to "break free" from the algorithm's grasp.

16   Homa Hosseinmardi et al., "Causally Estimating the Effect of YouTube's Recommender System Using Counterfactual Bots," *PNAS* 121, no. 8 (2024): e2313377121, doi.org/10.1073/pnas.2313377121.

To do this, researchers took one of their bot accounts that had a long history (120 videos) of watching far-right news and changed the bot's consumption to more moderate news channels for the next sixty videos. The findings surprised me. From the report:

> *If partisan consumers switch to moderate content, YouTube's sidebar recommender "forgets" their partisan preference within roughly thirty videos regardless of their prior history, while homepage recommendations shift more gradually toward moderate content.*

In the world of YouTube, thirty videos would equate to roughly six hours of viewing based on an average length of twelve minutes per video. For many people, this may not take long at all—a couple of days with consistent viewing and you could "reset" your algorithm. However, this study did not consider all of the other data points that YouTube would have on a typical user as part of the Google ecosystem. These bots did not have a documented history of search inquiries, emails, website logins via Google, tons of phone data from Android users, and more. With this data included, I am sure that it would take even longer than thirty videos to break free from the algorithm's hold.

If we apply some of that data to streaming apps and assume that they are using similar algorithms to YouTube and other entertainment apps, it is likely an even harder task to break free. Even if the streaming algorithms required less content, say ten to fifteen movies or TV shows to "break free," that is multiple days or weeks for the average user. It also would require a consistent shift, which might be even harder to do.

For example, say you had a month or two where you were on a big comedy kick. Every time you opened Netflix (picking on them because they are the biggest), you went straight to *I Think You Should Leave* or *Seinfeld* or *Arrested Development*. Naturally, the algorithm is going to recommend similar content to keep you engaged. But say October rolls around and you want some horror movies, or it's July and you are in the mood for some summer romance movies. Well, you won't see those recommended to you, even after several watches. And if you do jump back into *Seinfeld* in the middle of this shift, it will set the algorithm straight again.

There are ways to manually reset recommendations, usually in user settings, by deleting all of your existing history and starting fresh. But even then, you are served recommendations based on what's trending and popular amongst the masses. The reality is that you can't put people into a box, but that is what these algorithms want to do. Humans don't fit nicely into a single category. We are too complex for that. Algorithms will continue to improve and get "smarter," but as long as they rely on user input for their learning, it is so hard for a streaming service to make a solid recommendation or challenge you to try something new without being human and thinking outside the box.

Is it depressing? Sure. Scary? Yep. But luckily, we don't have to live that way. There are ways out of the bubble, and there are ways to break out of the algorithm and find movies that aren't trending. At the end of this book, I will have numerous ways for you to break free and explore cinema across all decades, genres, and countries. There are so many great movies out there, even from just the past decade, that you likely missed. And if you are a member of the younger millennial or Gen Z generations, even more "old" movies don't get nearly enough love from these algorithms because they aren't "sexy" and new. They don't drive clicks and new user sign-ups, so some of them disappear from the zeitgeist, which is too bad. Some of my favorite movies are from the 1970s, an amazing decade for film, yet you will almost never find them trending on major streaming services, if they are even available.

So, how did we get here? How did we go from a golden age of movies with theaters in every town and video stores on every corner to a world where we browse an endless sea of movie posters on our phones, computers, or smart TVs until we finally just watch *The Office* for the fifteenth time? Well, it is a long story, but one that starts with the shift in the types of movies that were made and the definition of success after the Streaming Revolution took hold of Hollywood.

1999 was a big year for movies. It had been sixteen years since the last movie in the original *Star Wars* trilogy, *Return of the Jedi*, had hit theaters. For years, fans of the saga had rewatched the original series over and over again. Every movie fan had a worn VHS copy of the trilogy somewhere, and hundreds of thousands of people flocked back to theaters for the special edition rerelease in 1997. *Star Wars* did almost $500 million at the box office for the original trilogy special edition rerelease. Adjust that for inflation, and it's $872 million in global ticket sales.[17] Those are insane numbers, and this was just a rerelease

17   Scott Mendelson, "20 Years Ago, *Star Wars: Special Edition* Made *Star Wars* Special Again," *Forbes*, February 1, 2017, forbes.com/sites/scottmendelson/2017/02/01/20-years-ago-star-wars-special-edition-made-star-wars-special-again.nne.

of a slightly edited (for better or worse, that's a whole different book) version of movies from years before. I don't think I need to tell movie fans that *Star Wars* was a big deal, so when a new trilogy was announced, fans were beyond excited.

Star Wars: Episode I—The Phantom Menace flew into theaters in 1999 and had fans racing to grab tickets faster than George Lucas making changes in the editing room. Opening night was chaos everywhere. Fans lined up days early, dressed as their favorite characters and waving lightsabers like they were doing their Jedi training exercises in the front lobby.

I was only seven years old at the time, but I remember the excitement. Everything was *Star Wars*. The fast-food restaurants had tie-ins. The vending machines were covered with artwork depicting young Anakin, Darth Maul, Obi-Wan, and Qui-Gon. You could not turn on the TV, drive down the road, open a newspaper, or get something to eat without seeing a promotion for the film. It felt special. It felt like an event. Because it was. In the world of movies, this was the biggest thing that had happened in years, and the whole world felt the effects of its reach.

This level of excitement wasn't always at the level of *Star Wars*, which is obviously a Hollywood juggernaut, but it wasn't all that uncommon either. Films like *Jurassic Park*, *Back to the Future*, *Scream*, *Titanic*, *Toy Story*, and so many others all captured the attention of the world when they were released. They were parodied in other movies and on shows like *Saturday Night Live*, the teams behind them were all over the talk show circuit, and the phenomenon lasted for months. These movies were made meticulously so that they would generate this level of cultural excitement, which would lead to huge box office returns over several months.

Before streaming and in the early days of home video, movies would routinely have three-to-six-month theatrical runs, giving as many people as possible a chance to see the hits on the big screen. The output of Hollywood was lower at this time, and it would not be uncommon for a film to be number one at the box office for weeks upon weeks.

It was also much more common for people to see movies multiple times, as they knew that it would be months before they could watch them at home. The availability of local theaters also helped with the access and availability of movies. In 1996, there were nearly 8,000 movie theaters across the United States. By 2020, that number had dropped below 6,000.[18] Recent estimates post-COVID-19 put the number somewhere around 5,500.[19] So, the market is mostly stabilized and did survive the pandemic by a thread (more on the impact of COVID-19 later), but that is still a loss of over 2,000 movie theaters in just twenty-five years. The theaters that closed were a lot of local small businesses that were pillars of communities for years but could not compete with the massive Cineplexes, upgraded technology required for digital movies, and of course, a smaller and smaller cut of ticket prices each year. Even driving around my small town in New Hampshire, I routinely come across two closed theaters that used to serve the community well and simply could not compete in the new world of entertainment.

On top of that, the long-term plan allowed the studios time to react. If they had a surprise hit on their hands, they had months to get out merchandise and additional marketing. If they knew it would hit, like *Jurassic Park*, they could roll out a multi-month marketing and merchandise plan that kept their movie top of mind for as long as they could maintain the momentum. And it worked. If you are my

18   Laura Carollo, "US: Annual Number of Cinema Sites 1995-2020," Statista, January 5, 2023, statista.com/statistics/188643/number-of-us-cinema-sites-since-1995.

19   Travis Clark, "How 6 Indie Theaters Adapted as the Pandemic Rocked the Movie Industry and Why Execs Are Hopeful for the Future," *Business Insider*, March 22, 2022, businessinsider.com/how-indie-theaters-survived-the-pandemic-and-what-comes-next-2022-3.

age, you will distinctly remember the *Jurassic Park* or *Star Wars* special edition merchandise flying off the shelves at big-box retailers across the world. Today, they sell for good money on eBay and are still extremely popular collectors' items.

When the theatrical run was over, they would transition right into home video, selling VHS tapes in the millions, making hundreds of millions of dollars more in revenue. Those tapes would then be on the shelves at rental stores for years, still dominating shelf space and getting major attention from customers long after they were released. The longtail success of home video sales and video rentals meant that a film did not have to make back its entire budget on its opening weekend. Movies could take their time in theaters and there wasn't as much panic in the industry knowing the financial opportunities that would come later.

On an episode of the popular talk show *Hot Ones* with host Sean Evans, actor Matt Damon was asked about the shifts in Hollywood since he broke in during the 1990s.[20] Damon laid out exactly why this happened, and it all comes back to home video and the shift away from physical media to streaming:

20   Matt Damon, "Matt Damon Sweats From His Scalp While Eating Spicy Wings | Hot Ones," hosted by Sean Evans, posted August 5, 2021, by First We Feast, YouTube, 27:18, youtu.be/yaXma6K9mzo.

*So, what happened was the DVD was a huge
part of our business, of our revenue stream.
Technology has just made that obsolete, and so
the movies that we used to make, you could afford
to not make all of your money when it played in
the theater because you knew you had the DVD
coming behind the release.*

In reference to his 2013 film *Behind the Candelabra*,
Damon continued:

*I talked to a studio executive who explained it
was a twenty-five-million-dollar movie. I would
have to put that much into print and advertising
to market it…so I'd have to put that in P&A, so
now I'm in fifty million dollars. I have to split
everything I get with the exhibitor, right, the
people who own the movie theaters, so I would
have to make 100 million dollars before I got into
profit, and the idea of making 100 million dollars
on a story about this love affair between these
two people… That's suddenly a massive gamble.*

For years, this was the Hollywood formula for success. The major players were making movies that would do well in this system. They were forced to focus on quality over quantity because they knew that it only took one *Jurassic Park* or *Star Wars* to blow away everyone else's movie for most of a year. The longtail of home video sales and rentals would keep movies in the limelight for months at a time. It created a competitive landscape that drove creativity and resulted in studios and movies that took far more risks and swung for the fences. Then, it all changed.

Hollywood has gone from silent movies to talkies, black-and-white to color, from widescreen cameras to Panavision and eventually IMAX, and from flat images to 3D experiences. Theaters sold tickets at the box office, then by mail, then by email, and then through online stores generating barcodes in an app. There has always been a lot of change in the business as technology progresses, as is the same with any business. But there has never been anything in the more than a hundred years of film that has changed the industry as dramatically as streaming. Streaming services truly changed Hollywood forever, because the formula for success shifted completely.

It wasn't an immediate shift when Netflix launched their online streaming service, but more of a gradual shift as more players entered the game and each studio began to build out a proprietary service to compete with the other nonaffiliated services. Now that we live in a world where everyone has a streaming service, the goalposts for success have moved.

A "successful" movie is no longer measured by just dollars but by attention and time. Every one of these services is competing for your attention and they know that to capture it, they need a constant stream of entertainment. The new model for success values total views, likes, and hours watched over tickets sold. They compete for stats on completion rates (how many people stuck around for the entire movie) and viewer retention (how many people stuck with a movie past the first ten minutes). It is no longer about creating a long-term cultural event or curating pieces of art that took years to come to the screen. It's about "content," that dirty word that you see everywhere now.

Books are content. Movies are content. Social media posts are content. Blogs and news sites are content. Art is content. Everything is made these days to be consumed quickly and easily so that you can move right on to the next thing and hopefully keep absorbing more content from the same source. If the source loses your attention and you move on to some other source of entertainment, they have lost.

So, let's go back to *Star Wars: Episode I—The Phantom Menace*. That movie was huge, because it was the first *Star Wars* movie in sixteen years! Some fans, like me, had grown up on the series but never had a chance to see one of the movies in theaters. It was a massive cultural moment for the world. The same effect was in play sixteen years later, when *Episode VII—The Force Awakens* released. That movie was massive, arguably bigger than the prequels because people had soured on those movies and their story, and this was the first "new" storyline in *Star Wars* history. It had its trailer premiere on Monday Night Football. It broke ticketing platforms when presales went live. The hype was insane. But today? We have had so many different *Star Wars* properties since then that many people can't keep up or simply don't care anymore.

Speaking from personal experience, I was still a huge fan throughout the prequel trilogy and all the way up through *Episode IX—The Rise of Skywalker*. I made sure I was tuned into that random Monday Night Football game in 2015, watching the countdown until they showed the trailer for *The Force Awakens*. Then we got *The Mandalorian*, and I tuned in every week for new episodes. Now? I am burned out. There is so much *Star Wars* out in the world that I got bored. It lost any sort of special feeling. And Disney made it seem as if you had to watch everything they released to understand what was coming next. They have locked people into a bubble of endless *Star Wars* content so that once one show or movie ends its run, another one is right behind it. It is *Star Wars* or bust. You were either all in or getting left behind. Unfortunately for previously passionate fans like me, many of us got left behind.

But this is not just a Disney problem, even though they have done the same with their Marvel IP (intellectual property, meaning the characters and stories that they own as part of Marvel) and the endless stream of content there. It is an industry problem. Every studio wanted their *Star Wars* so that they could fill your brain with TV shows, social media content, movies, and mini-series and keep feeding the online commentary channels that "react" to every piece of news about their favorite IP. They were all feeding into the machine. Whether it was *Star Wars* or the Marvel Cinematic Universe (MCU), *Lord of the Rings*, *The Fast and the Furious*, or *Halloween*, everyone was going with content overload and still is today. Everything needs a "universe" of content, and without it, Hollywood won't listen to your pitch. And if by chance you do squeeze out an original idea that does well, like *Stranger Things* or *Squid Game*, you should fully expect that to be milked until it is dry with spinoffs and expanded stories.

When the COVID-19 pandemic hit in 2020, that was one of the real catalysts to this shift. People were stuck at home, theaters were closed, and streaming was the main outlet for most of the world. We were all on our couches watching *Tiger King* in March 2020. The industry took notice and has tried to replicate that feeling and phenomenon ever since then. But think about it—when was the last time you really thought about *Tiger King* or the other "viral" phenomena that were going around the streaming services back then? It has probably been a while, because you were on to the next thing, and the next one, and the one after that...

So, while the industry has fundamentally changed how they approach entertainment and movies, we have also shifted our viewing habits. Our attention spans are shorter than ever because of social media and the content we consume on our phones. Everywhere you look, short-form content is dominating the world. TikTok, Instagram Reels, and Snapchat dominate the short-form landscape. Even long-form content channels, like YouTube, have shifted focus to "shorts." It is a major reason why, after almost eight years of grinding on YouTube, uploading over 1,000 long-form videos to their platform, that I have shifted to shorter content on social media. It is far easier to reach millions of people with a ninety-second video than it is to reach even 10 percent of that audience with a ten-minute video.

A lot of the content that gets consumed today is disposable. People are on from one video to the next quickly. If they don't like a movie, they shut it off and scroll through their app until they find something else to watch. On one hand, this is extremely convenient. We all have access to more movies and TV shows than we have ever had before. But it also lacks intention. When you went to a video store in 1995, you took your time and had to make the "right decision" because you weren't going to be back at the store for several days. If you started to watch a movie and didn't immediately like it, you still gave it a chance because it was your only option for the night. Sometimes it worked out, and sometimes it didn't. But that was all part of the movie-watching experience, and it was how you truly discovered what resonates with you as a movie fan.

Since the content is disposable, the major studios make movies that are also disposable. I hate to keep dumping on Disney, but when you are the biggest media and entertainment conglomerate in the world, it is easy to find flaws. Let's take the post-*Avengers Endgame* MCU as an example. Prior to *Endgame*, the trope of the post-credit scene cliffhanger that ties some small cameo or moment into the next film was still present. The MCU used this effectively in the *Avengers* saga to tease characters like Thanos, build hype for the next sequel, and eventually, let everything build up to what was probably the biggest cinematic event of the 2010s with *Avengers: Endgame*. It worked because it wasn't overdone.

Post-*Endgame*, the MCU continued this effort to build something larger. It worked for a while. *Spiderman: No Way Home* was the most fun I had had in theaters in a long time. But it got too big. Now the post-credit scenes might tie back to a mini-series on Disney+ or even a single episode of an anthology series. You need to watch all of those shows to keep up with the latest lore. And before you know it, you are in the Marvel bubble, right next to those people in the *Star Wars* bubble. If you are in both, all the power to you! But you must have a lot of time on your hands, because I can barely keep up with one.

Disney is not the only culprit, though. They are just the ones who have been successful. Universal tried to build a universe of Universal Monsters called "The Dark Universe" with films like *The Mummy* and *Dracula: Untold*. They lined up major stars like Tom Cruise, Russell Crowe, Javier Bardem, and Johnny Depp to star in a full slate of movies inspired by the classic Universal Monsters movies. After the disaster that was *The Mummy*, Universal essentially canceled these plans. But if it had worked and more audiences had come out to see *The Mummy*, we would likely be watching spin-off TV shows, countless sequels, and an interconnected universe not unlike the MCU.

If we look at Warner Brothers, they have *Harry Potter*. They already had eight successful films that spawned Potter-craze across the US, but that was not enough. Now there is a theme park (which looks like a lot of fun), spin-off movies like *Fantastic Beasts*, and a TV show that will break down each of the seven books into individual seasons.

There are numerous other examples of this, because Hollywood knows that this is what will make them money. They know that they can use psychology and the changes that the internet has made to our brains to suck people into a world so deep that they cannot escape. They crave the next thing as soon as they finish something else. It creates a cult-like mentality around these IPs that has unfortunately resulted in small pockets of toxic fanbases and online communities that occasionally lash out in horrible ways against people involved in these projects. IP is everything, and profits are tied to IP.

While I was researching for and writing this book, the final box office numbers for 2024 were released, and it is a fascinating look into the state of Hollywood today versus thirty years prior. In 2024, of the top twenty-five grossing films worldwide, only one, *If*, was a totally original film.[21] *If* barely squeaked in at twenty-fourth in the worldwide box office results. There were other films with adapted screenplays from books, like *The Wild Robot* and *It Ends With Us*, and sequels with original screenplays but existing IPs, like *Moana 2* and *Deadpool & Wolverine*, but *If* was the only film with a truly original script written from scratch. And unfortunately, it was deemed a box office failure based on its high budget.

If we go back thirty years to 1994, the box office results tell a different story.[22] Just looking at the top ten movies from that year, there are original stories like *True Lies*, *Pulp Fiction*, *Speed*, *Dumb and Dumber*, and *The Santa Clause* scattered throughout the top ten. If you expand to the top twenty-five, original films like *Stargate*, *Ace Ventura: Pet Detective*, *Wolf*, and *Four Weddings and a Funeral* round out the list. Nearly half of the top twenty-five grossing movies in 1994 were original screenplays, and even though this sounds unbelievable because of what we expect today,

21   "2024 Worldwide Box Office," Box Office Mojo, boxofficemojo.com/year/world/2024.

22   "1994 Worldwide Box Office," Box Office Mojo, boxofficemojo.com/year/world/1994.

there was only one sequel in the top twenty-five—*Naked Gun 33⅓: The Final Insult*.

It is clear that things have changed drastically. In modern Hollywood, IPs are required for major studios to make an investment. This could mean that your movie is a sequel or a remake of an existing IP. It could mean that your movie is tied to a video game franchise or a popular book series. It could mean that the movie is tied to a famous character, like Garfield or Scooby-Doo. But unless you are Martin Scorsese, Quentin Tarantino, Christopher Nolan, Denis Villeneuve, Steven Spielberg, or James Cameron, you need to have an existing consumer base and brand recognition built into your project. Otherwise, you better start looking for independent investors and hoping that one of the indie studios picks it up for distribution after a festival run.

So, you either need an IP, a lot of independent money and investors, or one of the indie distributors like A24 or NEON to buy into your film to get a wide release these days. But say you do have that as a filmmaker— will you be able to show it in a movie theater? I touched briefly on the changes that have affected theaters and audiences over the history of movies, but it is important to understand at a deeper level to fully comprehend the massive changes that are already in place due to

COVID-19 and the Streaming Revolution. Movie theaters are still my favorite way to watch a movie, but they may not be long for this world.

If you love movies, then you love movie theaters and the theatrical experience. There is nothing like seeing a movie on a giant screen with speakers filling every corner of the room. Whether it's a movie you have seen a dozen times or a new release that you know nothing about, I think we can all agree that there is a certain magic to the movie theater. It is an escape from reality for two hours, free from the distractions of the outside world. It is just you, an audience of other fans, a great story, a big screen, and a dark room. And for as long as there have been movies, there have been movie theaters.

They were there through wars, recessions, political and social uncertainty, and numerous health crises. They were unstoppable sources of revenue for Hollywood with theater chains worldwide raking in billions of dollars each year. 2019 was a record-breaking year for the global box office, as movies made more than $45 billion worldwide, with a near-record $11.4 billion (just behind 2018's record $11.9 billion) coming from just the

United States.[23] Then, COVID-19 reared its ugly head, and everything changed.

When COVID-19 first hit, nobody knew what to expect. In the early days of the pandemic in January and February 2020, movies were still heading to theaters and having success, even for a traditionally slow time for theatrical releases. *Bad Boys for Life* was released on January 17, 2020, and ended up grossing over $426.5 million worldwide.[24] This was the third largest January box office in history, and the movie industry looked like it was going to pick up in 2020 right where the 2010s left off.

As the worries around a potential pandemic grew, it still wasn't keeping people from the theaters. On February 12, 2020, about a month before the world shut down, *Sonic the Hedgehog* was released in theaters and became a surprise hit, grossing almost $320 million worldwide.[25] On February 26, *The Invisible Man* hit theaters. The film was an R-rated, modern take on the Universal Classic Monster character. An R-rated horror movie in late February? Not ideal for the box office. And yet, even with COVID-19 cases creeping up nationwide, *The Invisible*

23   "2019 Worldwide Box Office," Box Office Mojo, boxofficemojo.com/year/world/2019.

24   *"Bad Boys for Life* (2020)," Box Office Mojo, boxofficemojo.com/title/tt1502397.

25   *"Sonic the Hedgehog* (2020)," Box Office Mojo, boxofficemojo.com/title/tt3794354.

Man managed to gross nearly $145 million worldwide, including over $70 million in the United States with only a three-week window before theaters shut down.[26]

On March 16, 2020, AMC and Regal, two of the biggest movie theater chains, announced they were closing all of their locations to help curb the spread of the virus.[27] In the following hours and days, the rest of the country, and the world, followed suit. The movies were closed, and everyone was stuck inside.

None of us had experienced something at this level before. It is all burned into my memories. I remember where I was when I got the email on a Saturday night saying that we wouldn't be going to work on Monday morning (I have worked from home since). I remember the CBS Sports alert I got at a men's basketball game when the NBA shut down their season. I remember going to the last NHL game played in Boston before the season was canceled and looking around at the huge crowd, wondering who had COVID-19 and how far it would spread amongst the 20,000 people in the stadium. I remember sitting at my kitchen table with a laptop,

26   *"The Invisible Man* (2020)," Box Office Mojo, boxofficemojo.com/title/tt1051906.

27   Lauren Hirsch, "As L.A. Theaters Close Due to Coronavirus, AMC Reduces Capacity to 50%," *Los Angeles Times*, March 16, 2020, latimes.com/entertainment-arts/business/story/2020-03-16/as-l-a-theaters-close-due-to-coronavirus-amc-reduces-capacity-to-50.

not thinking I would ever need a more permanent work-from-home solution because we would all be back in the office after a week or two. And I distinctly remember when the movie theaters shut down and the movies I was highly anticipating, like *Top Gun: Maverick*, were pushed months, and eventually years, into the future. I remember shopping at an empty Jordan's Furniture store because we needed a new couch for our house, and using the bathrooms over by their empty IMAX theater, looking at the poster for *Top Gun: Maverick* with a June 26, 2020 release date. (If you aren't from the area, Jordan's is a furniture store, but also a sort of mini-attraction, with all sorts of extra activities like a trapeze station, indoor skydiving, a restaurant, and as mentioned, a full-sized IMAX theater.) Many strange things like this are easy to recall because they had such a massive impact on all of our lives.

We were all optimistic at the start of it all, and so was the movie theater industry. AMC and Regal originally planned to close only through March 31, following the now-infamous guidance that a two-week period would be enough to "flatten the curve." What began as two weeks became six months, and although some theaters were permitted to open again during the late summer of 2020 during a lull in the pandemic, they were limited in capacity as social distancing was still enforced. The industry was struggling to keep up with streaming and home entertainment options already, and COVID-19, for lack of a better term, shot them while they were down.

Worst of all, even though the Hollywood studios and theatrical chains had always been close partners, Hollywood would not wait around for the theaters to reopen. Once the studios realized that theaters were going to be closed for a while and they would be losing a huge part of their revenue, they quickly pivoted to at-home viewing options, leaving theater owners twiddling their thumbs and waiting for a vaccine. Theaters had to resort to selling their popcorn to make a few dollars and try to keep their doors open. I also remember renting out a small independent theater for our socially distanced Christmas in 2020, getting the whole place to ourselves and spreading out across the empty theater as we watched a DVD copy of *Jingle All the Way* and exchanged gifts from afar. It was truly all that these businesses could do without audiences and without content to show on their screens even when the partial audiences returned.

Hollywood is driven by money, and when they saw their pockets getting emptied by the pandemic, they made a quick shift to a model they started calling "premium rentals," offering movies that would have typically been theatrical exclusives for at-home rental. On March 16,

2020, the same day that AMC and Regal announced they were closing all of their theaters in the US, Universal Studios announced the premium rental option for three movies—*The Hunt*, *The Invisible Man*, and *Emma*. For $20, consumers could rent these movies at home for forty-eight hours through various services like Amazon Prime, iTunes, and cable services. This wasn't a new practice—movie rentals had been available on these services for years now. Movies had also skipped theatrical releases from time to time for decades—thousands of direct-to-video movies never saw a movie theater and went right to VHS or DVD. But this was different, because this was breaking the rules.

Theatrical release schedules are laid out months in advance, and there were specific windows in which the theater chains and studios would agree that a film would play exclusively in theaters before it went to home video, digital rental, and streaming. In the days before streaming, these windows were huge, and movies would remain in theaters for months before they left for home video. This gave movies much longer legs in the cultural zeitgeist, and it also allowed theaters to remain more profitable. Each week that went by after opening weekend meant a bigger cut for the theater, so there was an incentive for the theaters to keep showing the movies for as long as audiences would buy tickets. The studios didn't mind, because they knew that it was great for marketing and would lead to huge home video and merchandise sales. It was a win-win for everyone.

These years were a hard time for theaters, and the smaller ones were hit especially hard. Even with small business loans and the attempt at relief from the government, many of the smaller theaters that had been cornerstones of communities for decades did not survive the pandemic. According to The Cinema Foundation, there were 2,000 fewer movie screens in the US in 2023 compared to pre-pandemic numbers in 2020. While that only reflects a 5 percent decrease in the total available screens across the country, many of those missing screens were one- or two-screen independent theaters.[28] Hundreds of theaters closed in those three years, and many more are still struggling to stay afloat. Even major chains like AMC and Regal had to close locations, and it continues today.

In September 2024, my local AMC theater closed. Thankfully, it sounds like a local chain will be picking up the location and fixing it up, as AMC had let it go to waste over the last few years, but even in a suburban area of about 80,000 people, that AMC could not sustain itself. I would break out the world's smallest violin for

---

28   The Cinema Foundation, *State of the Cinema Industry* (The Cinema Foundation, 2023), thecinemafoundation.org/wp-content/uploads/2023/03/State-of-the-Cinema-Industry-March-2023.pdf.

all of these theaters if they were only major chains from billion-dollar companies, but smaller theaters in communities across the country that were not connected to a major chain were hit the hardest, and that is truly sad and discouraging.

COVID-19 was a serious hit to these community theaters, but there was also an even bigger hit about a decade earlier as well. When Hollywood first started to move to digital projection in 2009, independent theaters were forced to upgrade their equipment to show the latest releases. The conversion to digital projectors was estimated to cost between $50,000 to $100,000 in 2013, and that conversion would have to happen in every screening room.[29] Even one of those conversions could kill a local theater, and if they had more than one screen, they were looking at a huge bill in front of them. Back in 2012, experts were predicting that around 20 percent of the movie theaters in the US would close as a result of the digital conversion costs, which amounted to 10,000 screens.[30] The mantra from the National Association of Theatre Owners was pretty blunt—"Convert or die."

29   David Bordwell, "Pandora's Digital Box: From Films to Files," David Bordwell's Website on Cinema, February 28, 2012, davidbordwell.net/blog/2012/02/28/pandoras-digital-box-from-films-to-files.

30   Michael Hurley, "We're About to Lose 1,000 Small Theaters That Can't Convert to Digital. Does It Matter?," IndieWire, February 23, 2012, indiewire.com/features/craft/were-about-to-lose-1000-small-theaters-that-cant-convert-to-digital-does-it-matter-49209.

Although many small theaters closed, the impact was not as severe as COVID-19, as many smaller venues crowdfunded the conversion costs, took advantage of studio-funded support (the studios were saving millions on the conversion to digital from 35mm), or got grants from nonprofits and arts organizations to remain open. Those that did not make it were either closed temporarily until they could raise funds, or in many cases, taken over by a chain like AMC or Regal which could front the cost of conversion. Between 2009 and 2014 during the conversion to digital, the number of screens in the US remained flat, between 41,000 and 43,000.[31] While there is no way to be sure how many local theaters closed, the consensus is that there were hundreds that didn't make it or could not recoup the costs of digital conversion. It was minimal compared to the original prediction that we would lose 20 percent of theaters and over 1,000 screens, but it was still a major hit to independent theaters that would only get worse as the years went on.

As local theaters close, entire communities are losing access to the theatrical experience. I have always been fortunate enough to live in moderately populated suburban areas that have plenty of entertainment

31   Motion Picture Association of America, *Theatrical Market Statistics 2013* (Motion Picture Association of America, 2013), motionpictures.org/wp-content/uploads/2014/03/MPAA-Theatrical-Market-Statistics-2013_032514-v2.pdf.

options, but that is not the case for many people in the US and abroad. In rural areas of the United States, these local theaters would have been the lifeblood of the community when it comes to entertainment, offering residents a chance to see the latest releases on the big screen. As those opportunities dry up, it will inevitably lead to more hours spent on streaming instead of in a theater.

But maybe all of this is by design, meant to drive more business to the major players in Hollywood and less business to local theaters. If ticket sales continue the way they are going, even the biggest chains will be in trouble. Could the movie studios be making a play to control the distribution market entirely? I think so. If you don't mind putting on your aluminum foil helmet and getting into some conspiracies for a moment, the trends are certainly alarming.

When COVID-19 hit, it gave the big studios their first look at a world where they owned the entire distribution channel. They owned the initial release of films which went direct to people's homes, they kept all of that profit, and they felt pretty good. Even without the box office returns, the studios survived because they saw a massive influx in streaming subscriptions and VOD (video-on-demand) rentals. According to most industry knowledge, the average VOD rental from a service like

Apple TV, Prime Video, or Fandango at Home will net the studios a 70 percent share on each sale.[32] In comparison, theatrical ticket sales average between 50 and 60 percent share, although it can vary depending on the studio and project.[33] It may not seem like a huge difference, but it is when you are working with sales in the tens and hundreds of millions of dollars. Don't believe me? Let's do the math.

For the purposes of this equation, let's assume that a standard movie ticket is $12, and a premium (new release) rental is $20. When the movie is released to theaters, it sells four million tickets at $12 each, for a total of $48 million. Assuming the studio averages a 50 percent cut of the revenue, they will make $24 million on those ticket sales.

Now, let's assume they take the same movie but release it straight to VOD platforms at a premium rental price of $20. That may seem expensive, but keep in mind, that is not $20 per person. A family of four can watch that movie for $20 at home, or they can spend $48 plus concessions to see the movie in theaters. If the movie sells 2.4 million

---

32   Alexl Farber, "Faster Home Release for Films Shrinks Takings for Cinemas," *The Times*, April 23, 2025, thetimes.co.uk/article/faster-home-release-for-films-shrinks-takings-for-cinemas-3b9nt3lnb.

33   Dina Zipin, "How Exactly Do Movies Make Money?," Investopedia, updated October 1, 2024, investopedia.com/articles/investing/093015/how-exactly-do-movies-make-money.asp.

rentals at $20 each, the movie still makes $48 million. However, the studio takes 70 percent of that, meaning they make $33.6 million. So, they can sell 40 percent less "tickets" (rentals) and make 40 percent more dollars.

If you remove theaters from the equation, you may even sell more rentals and take in more rental sales than my conservative 40 percent difference from theater sales. We are talking about hundreds of millions of dollars more profit for the studios if they own more of the distribution channels. You can see where sharing with theater chains started to make less sense. There is an incentive to bring that revenue share up to 70 percent or more in a world where shareholders are breathing down the necks of these public companies and asking for more growth every year.

If they did not have their own streaming service (like Sony, or Paramount at the time), they sold the streaming rights of new movies to services like Netflix or Amazon Prime for huge sums of money. For example, it was reported that Paramount sold *Coming 2 America* to Amazon for $125 million.[34] I honestly don't know that a legacy comedy sequel like that would have even made that much in theaters, so that seems like a huge win.

34   Rebecca Rubin, "Hefty Streamer Deals: COVID Pandemic Theater Shutdowns,"
      Variety, April 15, 2020, variety.com/2020/film/features/hefty-streamer-deals-
      covid-pandemic-theater-shutdowns-1234848687.

I think they got a taste of this new world and realized that they could be making a lot more money without a middleman, especially when theaters reopened. In a capitalist cutthroat business like entertainment, they saw an opportunity, and they started to make plans to shift toward this new bucket of gold they found at the bottom of the COVID-19 rainbow. Here is where my mild conspiracy theory begins.

When the studios saw what they could get away with in terms of digital rentals and streaming during COVID-19, they planned to own the entire entertainment funnel. First step—kill off the movie theaters and buy them when they go bankrupt. It may sound crazy, but look at recent trends and the way that major studios are approaching theatrical releases. The theatrical window has shrunk significantly over the last twenty years.

Go back to the early 2000s, and you could be waiting months before you could watch a movie at home on VHS or DVD, and months more after that before you could watch a movie on HBO or one of the basic cable networks like on ABC's Sunday Night Movie program. Streaming and on-demand options did not come around until later, and theaters would have multiple weeks and months to ride the hot sales of big-ticket movies. However, recent agreements between movie studios and theaters have turned the industry on its head. In July 2020, Universal signed what I would consider to be a landmark theatrical distribution deal with the major theater chain AMC Theatres and followed that up with the same agreement with the chain Cinemark in November 2020. These are the two largest theater chains in the world, and the deal would change theaters forever. From the official Universal statement,[35] the guidelines are below:

The agreement includes at least three full weekends (seventeen days) of theatrical exclusivity for all Universal Pictures and Focus Features theatrical releases, at which time the studio will have the option to make its titles available across premium video on demand (PVOD) platforms. Under the terms of the deal, any title that opens to $50 million or more, including many franchise titles, will play exclusively in theaters for at least five full weekends (thirty-one days) before the title may become available on PVOD.

35   "Universal Filmed Entertainment Group and Cinemark Theaters Announce Dynamic Release Window Agreement for Exhibition of Universal Films," Business Wire, November 16, 2020, ir.cinemark.com/news-events/press-releases/detail/478/universal-filmed-entertainment-group-and-cinemark-theaters.

Seventeen days is not a lot of time. But that is all that is guaranteed for any movie that makes under $50 million on its opening weekend—quite a few "big" movies. For example, during the weekend that I am writing this, *Smile 2* became the number one movie in America, grossing $23 million.[36] That's a great number for a mid-budget horror movie, but it also means that you can expect it to be available to rent at home in just about two weeks from its opening weekend. If you don't see a movie in the first two weeks, there is no point in going to the theater for anything other than the experience, which is also an issue (more on that later). The exclusivity that movie theaters enjoyed for decades is essentially gone. Unless you are Christopher Nolan or James Cameron with the heavyweight power to force the studios to keep movies in theaters longer per contractual agreements, most movies will be available at home in two weeks, and the bigger hits in thirty days.

This is a direct attack against the theatrical experience in my opinion, especially since the theaters' revenue share increases each subsequent week of a movie's release. And the theaters are hurting majorly from this. AMC reported in Q2 of 2024 that their revenue was down

36   *"Smile 2,"* Box Office Mojo, boxofficemojo.com/release/rl665813761.

23.5 percent.[37] Cinemark reported a drop of 15.4 percent during the same time.[38] Some of this is seasonal, and the second half of 2024 has big movies that could provide a boost. But both chains have still not recovered to pre-pandemic numbers, even as inflation and market trends have shifted ticket prices and concessions to the highest level we have ever seen. People are going to the movies less, and the major studios are not helping their cause.

It may take some years, but I think the collapse of the current theatrical system is inevitable. So what is their endgame? Why would the studios want to kill the theaters? Well, I think it may look something like what Sony did with Alamo Drafthouse.

In June 2024, Sony shocked the world by acquiring Alamo Drafthouse, an extremely popular, albeit small, movie theater chain. This is the first time in history that a major studio like Sony has owned their theaters, which signals a major shakeup in the way theaters are run. Now, don't get me wrong, I like Sony (as previously mentioned, they do amazing work for physical media fans), and I love that they saved Drafthouse, because it is an awesome theater

37 Radek Strnad, "Leisure Facilities Stocks Q2 in Review: AMC Entertainment (NYSE:AMC) vs. Peers," Yahoo Finance, October 21, 2024, finance.yahoo.com/news/leisure-facilities-stocks-q2-review-065908134.html.

38 "Cinemark Holdings, Inc. Reports Second Quarter 2024 Results," Business Wire, August 2, 2024, ir.cinemark.com/news-events/press-releases/detail/601/cinemark-holdings-inc-reports-second-quarter-2024-results.

chain that struggled without a larger financial supporter and partner. But this is exactly what I expect to happen with AMC, Cinemark, Regal, and the other chains.

When they begin to truly struggle and need a bailout to avoid bankruptcy and further theater closures, do not be surprised if Disney, Warner Brothers Discovery, Comcast (owns NBC Universal), or even a tech company that has an interest in entertainment like Apple or Amazon jumps in to save them. If I were a betting man, I would have no problem putting money down on at least some, if not all, of these theater chains being scooped up by another entertainment or tech company within the next decade. It is a no-brainer move, and everything that the executives are talking about and the moves they are making regarding film distribution seems to point this way. But this isn't because the studios don't support theaters. For example, when David Zaslav, CEO of Warner Brothers Discovery, was asked his thoughts about upcoming films and their release strategy at CinemaCon in 2023, he said:[39]

At Warner Bros., at DC Studios, we believe that everything is possible. This business could be

39   Matt Donnelly, "David Zaslav Reassures Theater Owners: 'We're in No Rush to Bring the Movie to Max,'" *Variety*, April 26, 2023, variety.com/2023/film/news/david-zaslav-theatrical-movies-cinemacon-windows-1235594027.

> *bigger and stronger than it's ever been. We*
> *believe in full windowing of the motion pictures.*
> *We do not want to do direct-to-streaming movies.*
> *We're in no rush to bring the movie to Max.*

Other executives have echoed these statements. They believe in the theatrical experience. They believe it could be bigger and stronger than ever before, even with the current trends. But what they aren't saying is that they would love to own that revenue stream 100 percent, and they have the resources to do it.

In 2023, AMC Theatres brought in $4.8 billion in revenue.[40] Cinemark brought in just over $3 billion.[41] Compare that to Disney ($89 billion),[42] Warner Brothers Discovery ($41.3 billion),[43] Netflix ($33.8 billion),[44]

40   Laura Carollo, "AMC Theatres' Revenue 2013–2024," Statista, February 28, 2025, statista.com/statistics/206959/revenue-of-amc-theatres.

41   Laura Carollo, "Cinemark Holdings, Inc.'s Revenue 2006–2024," Statista, March 19, 2025, statista.com/statistics/207084/revenue-of-cinemark-since-2006.

42   The Walt Disney Company, *Fiscal Year 2023 Annual Financial Report* (The Walt Disney Company, 2024), thewaltdisneycompany.com/app/uploads/2024/02/2023-Annual-Report.pdf.

43   "Warner Bros. Discovery Revenue 2010–2025," Macrotrends, macrotrends.net/stocks/charts/WBD/warner-bros-discovery/revenue.

44   "Netflix Revenue 2010–2025," Macrotrends, macrotrends.net/stocks/charts/NFLX/netflix/revenue.

Paramount ($29.6 billion)[45] or tech juggernauts with entertainment interests like Amazon ($575 billion),[46] Apple ($383 billion),[47] Sony ($89 billion),[48] or Comcast ($121 billion).[49] Buying out AMC and Cinemark would be a significant financial commitment, but it is within reach for all of these companies. Sony buying up Drafthouse is not a one-time thing. It is the beginning of a trend.

When Warner or Disney or Amazon or Netflix own all the movie theaters and they are pulling in 100 percent of those profits by showing their original content, the growth numbers will look great to investors, because then things will change again. Theatrical windows will increase as each studio holds its properties in its theater chains for as long as it can to maximize profit and bring back the exclusivity that theaters enjoyed before. When that runs its course, they still get to sell plenty of rentals and streaming subscriptions to their services, and hopefully, physical media as well. These

45   "Paramount Global Revenue 2010–2024," Macrotrends, macrotrends.net/stocks/charts/PARA/paramount-global/revenue.

46   "Amazon Revenue 2010–2024," Macrotrends, macrotrends.net/stocks/charts/AMZN/amazon/revenue.

47   "Apple Revenue 2010–2024," Macrotrends, macrotrends.net/stocks/charts/AAPL/apple/revenue.

48   "Sony Revenue 2010–2024," Macrotrends, macrotrends.net/stocks/charts/SONY/sony/revenue.

49   "Comcast Revenue 2010–2025," Macrotrends, macrotrends.net/stocks/charts/CMCSA/comcast/revenue.

media conglomerates will own the entire movie business vertical, and they will get rich in the process.

Honestly, I hope that I am wrong. I am a firm believer in competition in all markets. It drives innovation and avoids the complacency that monopolies tend to create for the companies in charge of them. But everything seems to be lining up toward this future, and these big studios and tech companies are minding their time while the current theatrical system collapses. When it comes back together after a few acquisitions, we will be living in interesting times for movie fans.

If Disney buys a theater chain, will they show movies from Paramount and Warner Brothers? What would the others do if they were in the same position? Ultimately, I think they would be forced to show content from everyone. Sony certainly isn't limiting Drafthouse to content from Sony Pictures. That sort of limitation would be a death sentence for a theater chain. There isn't enough content to keep theaters open if they are exclusive to a single studio, no matter how large that studio is. But there will be weird things happening.

Would Disney withhold movies from theaters if Warner Brothers owned them, opting instead to put them straight on Disney+ rather than pay a cut to a competitor? Would Netflix start showing movies in theaters if they owned them, adding another revenue stream to their business, or is the sub-$10 billion box office business not worth it for a company of their size? There are a ton of questions and if and when it happens, I think there could be an entire book about the complications that arise. I think it is inevitable, so keep an eye on this space, but I also don't think that it solves the major issue that movie theaters have in the age of streaming: the battle against convenience.

For movie theaters to survive in this new world of entertainment, they have to find ways to build back the premium experience that movie theaters used to offer. Going to the movies has to become an event again. It has to become something special. But with endless entertainment options available to audiences at home, premier television shows like *Stranger Things* and *Game of Thrones* challenging movies for audience attention spans like never before, and in-theater audiences being more distracting than ever, there have to be a lot of changes to the industry.

As great as some of the new promotions have been, I do not see them moving the needle when it comes to ticket sales. For example, the new big thing in the movie theater world is the limited-edition popcorn bucket. Theaters have always had some sort of promotional cups and popcorn buckets with branded materials on them, but the industry reached new heights with the viral popularity of the *Dune: Part Two* sandworm bucket. Although it went viral for reasons they may not have expected—its hilarious design was either marketing geniuses at work, or a total accident—it drove a ton of interest for movie theaters and that movie. It was so popular that *Saturday Night Live* had a whole skit devoted to it and it spawned dozens of viral videos and memes that took the internet by storm.

And it worked! According to Box Office Mojo, *Dune: Part Two* grossed over $714 million worldwide.[50] In comparison, *Dune: Part One*, a massive success, only grossed $407 million worldwide.[51] Was it all about the popcorn bucket? Of course not. *Dune* had a huge following before the first movie was released, and it only grew with the great reviews and word of mouth from the first film. It also left audiences with a cliffhanger that was set to be settled in *Part Two*, so it was heading toward success well before the popcorn bucket.

As great as that promotion was, now it seems that every big-ticket movie, from *Deadpool & Wolverine* and *Alien: Romulus* to *Venom: The Last Dance* and *Beetlejuice, Beetlejuice* has a promotional popcorn bucket. The

---

50   *"Dune: Part Two,"* Box Office Mojo, boxofficemojo.com/title/tt15239678.

51   *"Dune: Part One,"* Box Office Mojo, boxofficemojo.com/title/tt1160419.

additional revenue for theaters has been incredible. Nels Storm, AMC Theatres' vice president of food and beverage product strategy, was quoted in an article from Today.com that AMC's merchandise sales had risen from "$0 five years ago (2018) to $54 million in 2023."[52] Those numbers are insane, but are they leading to more ticket sales?

Based on the numbers from industry reports that I covered earlier, I would have to say no. Ticket sales are still struggling, and since the rise of the popcorn bucket phenomenon in 2023, they have not improved. Other factors tie into this, and maybe without the buckets' sales they would be even worse. But based on what I have seen online as someone pretty tied into the movie collector community, a lot of people are buying the popcorn buckets as collectors, but not necessarily as a supplement to their ticket. I am sure many of these super fans and collectors like me also went to see the movie, but I cannot imagine that the popcorn buckets are what brought them there. In fact, I have seen many cases where people are driving to the theater to buy the buckets and then leaving without seeing a movie, and many more cases where resellers hit the online stores

52   Joseph Lamour, "*Gladiator II* Popcorn Bucket Is the Latest Movie Theater Collectible," *Today*, April 23, 2025, today.com/food/trends/gladiator-ii-popcorn-bucket-rcna176817.

hard on release day and throw the buckets up on eBay for a 300 percent markup. So, while it is nice for the theaters to bring in more revenue, it isn't necessarily helping their core business.

One thing I believe would go a long way to help theaters is to focus on their technological advantages again. Unless you are a multi-millionaire, chances are you do not have a thirty-foot-tall screen in your house. Even if you were that rich, the chances are even lower that you have something like a 100-foot-tall IMAX screen. According to Dolby, their Atmos experiences have sixty-four speakers in each theater. I know some people with incredible home theaters, but nobody can touch sixty-four speakers and a 100-foot screen. Sure, the average consumer can now purchase a large 4K TV for under $1,500, or even a 4K projector and a 150-inch screen for a few thousand dollars more. New home theater audio receivers can handle up to thirteen speakers and multiple subwoofers. But movie theaters will always have that advantage over the average consumer home theater, even as home theater technology progresses, because of their size and the immersive experience they offer.

Your home theater may feel immersive, and I agree, it can be. But nobody can tell me that they would rather watch *2001: A Space Odyssey* on a 4K Blu-ray disc at home when there are theaters showing 70mm prints of the same film. Having done both, I choose the movie theater experience ten times out of ten. It is that much better—if it is done right.

The best comparison I can make to the current situation with chain theaters is the chain restaurant and casual dining industry. We all know that when we go into a restaurant like Olive Garden or Applebee's, we aren't getting the same experience as locally owned restaurants with a dedicated chef. These chains all run like a machine, a step above fast food in some ways. They deliver a cheap dining experience with a menu that has something for everyone. They can be great for families looking for an inexpensive night out with picky kids. I have no issue with them! They serve a purpose, and they give people access to table service and dining out without breaking the bank. But they are suffering from the same issues that chain theaters are, and that is that the experience is failing.

The restaurants are understaffed, the quality of the food has dipped in recent years, and people are being enticed to stay home with easy delivery services like Uber Eats and DoorDash and food preparation packages like Hello Fresh and Blue Apron. Is the entire restaurant industry doomed? No, of course not. Neither is the entire movie theater industry. But it is changing, and people will spend their hard-earned money on a more premium experience. This means that they may go out less to restaurants or theaters, but it means that they will spend more and choose venues that deliver the experience they expect.

Convenience is no longer a winning formula for these businesses. Having hundreds of locations with ten to twenty screens in every major suburban area is not a selling point. We all have five screens in our homes with access to thousands of movies, the audience is typically more respectful (even if the kids are loud, at least they are your kids and you can shush them), the popcorn and snacks are cheaper, and you know the technology will work to your standards. At this point, it is truly at a point where theaters need to "convert or die" once again, and the ones that convert will be the ones that remain successful in this ever-changing world of movies and entertainment. But at the end of the day, the conversion may not even matter if the current Hollywood executives get their way.

As previously mentioned, movies fall into two categories today: big blockbuster, IP-driven movies with $200 million budgets, or independent movies with smaller budgets. The days of the $20 million studio movie are essentially gone. The Big Five studios will not take a risk on an original mid-budget movie, but they will continuously take the risk on films with a $200 million budget. To use a baseball analogy, it seems that Hollywood is always looking for a home run (*Avatar, Deadpool and Wolverine, Barbie*) and the only alternative at those budgets is a strikeout (*Borderlands, Jungle Cruise, The Flash*). And although that is not a successful strategy in baseball or in the movie industry, they have stuck with it over the last several decades.

For example, Warner Brothers hit a home run in 2023 with *Barbie*. Even with a $145 million production budget, at least the same amount in marketing budget,[53] licensing fees (Mattel, the owner of Barbie, took 5 percent of box office plus a percentage of profits)[54] and massive payouts to the cast (Margot Robbie earned a reported $50 million for the role),[55] *Barbie* easily made Warner Brothers hundreds of millions of dollars in profits after its $1.4 billion box office return,[56] merchandising, and VOD

53   Will Richards, "*Barbie*'s Marketing Budget Was More Than It Cost to Make the Film," *NME*, July 24, 2023, nme.com/news/film/barbie-marketing-budget-more-than-production-3472627.

54   Adam Starkey, "Here's How Much Mattel Will Earn from *Barbie* in 2023," *NME*, September 11, 2023, nme.com/news/film/heres-how-much-mattel-earn-barbie-in-2023-3496059.

55   Brent Lang and Matt Donnelly, "*Barbie*'s Big Payday: Margot Robbie Will Earn $50 Million in Salary and Box Office Bonuses," *Variety*, August 15, 2023, au.variety.com/2023/film/news/barbie-pay-margot-robbie-salary-box-office-bonuses-10898.

56   "*Barbie*," Box Office Mojo, boxofficemojo.com/release/rl1077904129.

and physical media sales. However, in the same year, Warner Brothers lost an estimated $200 million on *The Flash*, and another $113 million on *Blue Beetle*.[57] So, they hit a home run, but their strikeouts on the DC Extended Universe (DCEU) movies almost wiped out all of the gains from *Barbie*.

I can't say for sure that they would have been better off making smaller movies, or spending less, but it seems like common sense and basic math to me. It is a lot easier to recoup a $10 million budget than a $100 million budget. *The Flash* made over $271 million at the box office and still lost $200 million.[58] A $10 million movie only needs $30 million at the box office to be a success.[59] Cord Jefferson, writer and director of *American Fiction* (estimated $3–$5 million budget, $22.5 million at the box office)[60] said it

---

57   Sam Hargrave, "Warner Bros. Suffers Record-Breaking Box Office Losses from DC Movies," The Direct, August 30, 2023, thedirect.com/article/warner-bros-box-office-dc-movies-losses.

58   Sam Hargrave, "Warner Bros. Suffers Record-Breaking Box Office Losses from DC Movies," The Direct, August 30, 2023, thedirect.com/article/warner-bros-box-office-dc-movies-losses.

59   Ryan Scott, "Box Office Hit or Box Office Bomb? A Rough Guide to the Mysteries of Movie Math," SlashFilm, updated January 15, 2023, slashfilm.com/1168078/box-office-hit-or-box-office-bomb-a-rough-guide-to-the-mysteries-of-movie-math.

60   *"American Fiction* (2023)," The Numbers, the-numbers.com/movie/American-Fiction-%282023%29.

best in his Oscars acceptance speech after winning Best Adapted Screenplay:[61]

I understand that this is a risk-averse industry, I get it, but $200 million movies are also a risk. And it doesn't always work out, but you take the risk anyway. Instead of making one $200 million movie, try making twenty $10 million movies. Or fifty $4 million movies.

I 100 percent agree with Jefferson's statement, and I think it points to the direction the movie industry needs to take to recover from the current system which is focused on big profits and even bigger losses. The indie darlings like A24 and NEON are doing things the way they used to be done, keeping budgets small, telling compelling stories, and connecting with audiences through unique marketing campaigns. They aren't making billions of dollars on a single movie, but I would bet that they are more profitable than the major studios. Even when they go "big" and bust, like with A24's *Beau Is Afraid* ($35

---

61   Samantha Bergeson, "Cord Jefferson's Mid-Budget Plea to Hollywood: 'Try Making 20 $10 Million Movies' Instead of Blockbusters," IndieWire, March 11, 2024, indiewire.com/news/breaking-news/cord-jefferson-oscars-more-mid-budget-movies-1234963015.

million estimated loss)[62] or NEON's *Ferrari* (more than a $50 million loss),[63] they still have enough smaller hits to weather that storm. A big success like *Hereditary* ($83 million box office on a $10 million budget)[64] or *Longlegs* ($109 million box office on a reported $8–$10 million budget)[65] pays for their next ten movies.

Their success rates remain high because they take smart risks and don't have inflated budgets that Hollywood just can't seem to shake. It doesn't matter what your name is. You could be Margot Robbie, Brad Pitt, Tom Cruise, Leonardo DiCaprio, Nicole Kidman—you aren't getting $20–$30 million salaries to star in these films. If you want to star in one of their projects, you take a smaller salary or you take a profit share on the back end. If you want to work with A24 or NEON, you won't get a tie-in with Chevrolet or a commercial during the Super Bowl. You will get smart guerilla marketing through social media that remains cost-effective.

62   Jordan Ruimy, "*Beau Is Afraid* Had Losses of $35 Million," World of Reel, October 11, 2023, worldofreel.com/blog/2023/10/11/xz9cpqsd3s23u7oic739x1870lw9zq.

63   Charles Barfield, "Michael Mann Isn't Bothered by Low Box Office for *Ferrari*: 'I'm Confident in the Film's Long-Term Relevance,'" The Playlist, July 17, 2024, theplaylist.net/michael-mann-isnt-bothered-by-low-box-office-for-ferrari-im-confident-in-the-films-long-term-relevance-20240717.

64   "*Hereditary* (2018)," Box Office Mojo, boxofficemojo.com/release/rl2575288321.

65   Adam Blevins, "*Longlegs* Just Broke a Major 2024 Box Office Record," Collider, August 16, 2024, collider.com/longlegs-global-box-office-100-million.

The insane amount of financial bloat in Hollywood is what is leading to the home-run-or-bust mentality. They have to make billions because they are spending billions. And unfortunately, the studios are currently run by huge conglomerates and business people who are in it for the money and not for the art. Art needs to make money to continue being made. I don't have an issue with that—artists should be paid for their work and paid better if their art does well. I am not okay with pure greed, and that is where we are at with current studio leadership.

Greed is killing the major studios and the Hollywood system. They are making movies for shareholders, not for audiences. And it sucks, because there are so many people working for the studios that are still in it for the art, that truly care about the history of film and the legacy of studios like Paramount and Warner Brothers. The filmmakers are the same—they want to make good movies, they want to have control, but many times nowadays the director becomes not much more than a figurehead for the production while the studio executives pull the strings behind the scenes. Again, no issue there. If someone offered me $20 million to direct some soulless franchise film and I knew it could fund my next five passion projects, I would take it too. Get the money while it's still good, right? But I don't see it being sustainable. And this is all without mentioning streaming, and the damage that the current streaming distribution system is doing to the industry.

Streaming services have spent equally insane amounts of money over the last decade to one-up each other and attract the biggest stars, directors, and more subscribers. The running joke for a while was that Netflix would acquire pretty much anything and pay huge amounts of money for shows and movies because they were in a content race against Hollywood and other emerging platforms. An episode of *South Park* from 2017 (season twenty-one, episode four, "Franchise Prequel") skewered Netflix, franchise media, and Hollywood around the idea that Netflix would greenlight anything. At one point, Cartman says, "Netflix is starving for new shows right now... They will literally buy anything people pitch them."[66] Matt Parker and Trey Stone, the creators of *South Park*, have certainly been around show business long enough to share their true thoughts on the streaming phenomenon, and they were clearly onto something in their criticism.

As other services ramped up and did the same, it fed into the notion that the art of movies was slowly becoming a burn-and-churn type of system, much like social media,

66   South Park Digital Studios, *South Park*, season 21, episode 4, "Franchise Prequel," Comedy Central, originally aired October 18, 2017, directed by Trey Parker, written by Trey Parker and Matt Stone.

YouTube, podcasts, and other new forms of digital entertainment. There was less focus on quality and more focus on quantity, which meant that the production value and effort that went into the movies and shows that the platforms acquired varied. For every *Stranger Things*, *Roma*, *Beasts of No Nation*, or *Mindhunter* (if David Fincher is reading this, I am begging for another season), there were a dozen cheaply made shows and movies that would have had a hard time selling to the Syfy Channel or Hallmark Channel. But Netflix wanted content, and they spent billions of dollars getting it. Originally, that was through acquisitions of other catalogs, but as the 2010s ended, they shifted to original content produced in-house. In 2017, Netflix spent a reported $6.3 billion on content.[67] By 2021, that number was over $17 billion.[68] Cartman was right—if you wanted a project to get the green light, you needed to pitch to Netflix.

However, since 2021, Netflix has plateaued its spending on content for both originals and catalog acquisitions. In 2023, after the Hollywood strikes, Netflix dropped its

67   Rani Molla, "Netflix Spends More on Content Than Anyone Else on the Internet—and Many TV Networks, Too," *Vox*, February 26, 2018, vox.com/2018/2/26/17053936/how-much-netflix-billion-original-content-programs-tv-movies-hulu-disney-chart.

68   Rachyl Jones, "Netflix Will Spend 'Vast Majority' of Its $17 Billion Content Budget on Originals in 2024, Despite a Deluge of Licensed Hit Shows Up for Grabs," *Fortune*, April 25, 2024, fortune.com/2024/04/25/netflix-spending-budget-originals-licensing-content-shows-streaming.

budget to $12 billion. In 2024, they were shooting for a $17 billion budget again but have yet to match their spending total from 2021 since they had that record year.[69] Since Netflix remains the gold standard for streaming, it is easy to use it as a general guide for the rest of the industry. If they aren't spending as much, you can bet that others aren't either.

Apple TV+ is a great example of what I would consider to be an abject failure. Since its launch, Apple has spent over $20 billion in producing original content and acquisitions.[70] However, the most recent stats show that Apple TV+ generates less viewing in one month than Netflix does in one day.[71] That $20 billion earned them 0.8 percent of the US TV market[72]—a terrible investment of time and money from a typically strong company that usually makes good decisions or at least cuts the bad losses early. Warner-Discovery is in the same boat, with

69   "Netflix to Hike Content Spend to $17 Billion in 2024," *Business Today*, October 19, 2023, businesstoday.in/technology/news/story/netflix-to-hike-content-spend-to-17-billion-in-2024-402560-2023-10-19.

70   Scharon Harding, "Apple TV+ Spent $20B on Original Content. If Only People Actually Watched," *Ars Technica*, November 19, 2024, arstechnica.com/apple/2024/11/apple-tv-spent-20b-on-original-content-if-only-people-actually-watched.

71   Lucas Shaw, "Apple Tries to Rein In Hollywood Spending After Years of Losses," *Bloomberg*, July 21, 2024, bloomberg.com/news/newsletters/2024-07-21/apple-tries-to-rein-in-hollywood-spending-after-years-of-losses.

72   Stuart Heritage, "Big Stars, Little Shine: Is Anyone Actually Watching Apple TV+ Shows?" *The Guardian*, March 21, 2025, theguardian.com/tv-and-radio/2025/mar/21/apple-show-audience.

recent reports from industry insiders saying that they are considering splitting off their streaming and movie business from their TV business. That merger never made much sense to me, and even after all of the money spent on original programming for Max and Discovery, they aren't seeing the business results of their failing merger.

As these budgets get cut and acquisitions dry up, it has put many filmmakers in a difficult position. The streaming system was already incredibly unfriendly to many filmmakers, especially those working on indie films or in the documentary space. I have talked with many filmmakers and producers over the years that I have been involved with in making content around the film industry, and they all share similar concerns when it comes to streaming. The streamers did not share viewing numbers, they did not share revenue, and they were not helpful in letting filmmakers see the types of people who might be interested in their projects. It was an analytics black hole, which for someone running a business and trying to make a living as a filmmaker is a disaster.

Whether your movie was viewed 10,000 times or ten million times, you got your acquisition fee and that was it. There was no revenue share like a film with a theatrical release. Typically, it was a flat rate across the board, so there was not a huge incentive to do a "good job" with a film. Unless your name was Martin Scorsese or David Fincher, completed projects got roughly the same acquisition fee, and that led to many discouraged directors and artists who knew they were up against big content machines who were out for a quick payday versus making something they believed in.

As the budgets have started to dry up, the acquisition fees have gotten even smaller, and more independent filmmakers have started to move toward other platforms like YouTube, where at least they get a share of ad revenue if they have a big hit on their hands. One of the big viral movie hits in 2024 was *Milk & Serial*, a found-footage horror movie released by the comedy group That's A Bad Idea on their YouTube channel, completely free for anyone to watch. The film was made for just $800, and with 1.7 million views and counting, they probably made $10,000 to $20,000 on that movie with YouTube ad sharing.[73] But they also gained thousands of new subscribers, plenty of new fans, and industry attention that they may not have had by having the movie buried on a streaming platform or released to a free service like Tubi.

73   "How Much Money Do You Make Per View on YouTube?" Thinkific, thinkific.com/blog/youtube-money-per-view.

Other platforms like Vimeo or Kickstarter have become more popular as well, where filmmakers can sell access to their private movie links and get a cut of the earnings that way. Even newer platforms like Olyn are taking things one step further, allowing creators to post their movies for sale on a direct-to-consumer platform without a big corporate middleman like Prime Video or Apple TV taking their cut. Plus, they share the full analytics and email lists of the people who pay to watch the movie, so filmmakers can build themselves an audience for future projects.

The democratization of Hollywood through these new platforms and alternative media outlets is an interesting new shift in filmmaking that will surely lead to more independent films getting attention and finding audiences. It is a good thing for creatives, but it will mean that it is harder to attract audiences to films, which is another reason I am such a huge proponent of getting movie recommendations outside of the algorithm. Word of mouth and communities have driven independent films since the days of *Halloween*, and I feel like we are reentering a golden age of independent films driven by online communities, content creators, social media, and of course, good old word of mouth, even if that is by text or DM these days.

When I look at the biggest success stories of 2024, I don't look at a movie like *Dune: Part Two* or *Deadpool and Wolverine*. We all knew those movies would make a bunch of money. I am more excited about the success of movies like *Strange Darling*, *The Substance*, *Anora*, *Love Lies Bleeding*, and *Longlegs*. A movie like *The Substance* had no chance in the Hollywood machine of today—it was risky, it didn't have a trending A-list star (no offense to Demi Moore; she was brilliant and is a legend, but she is not the same box office pull she was in the '90s), it told a wholly original story, and it was off-the-wall bonkers. It is the type of movie I have enjoyed for years but often found a niche audience of only the most hardcore cinephiles. But something now feels different. I mentioned watching it around my parents, and even they had heard of it. For a couple of people who always tell me I watch weird stuff that no one else sees (my dad loves to make fun of the supposed "Scandinavian torture horror" I watch), I was shocked to hear they even recognized the movie by name, never mind that they even knew what it was about!

I know that I am relaying personal experiences here that could be biased and filtered through my rose-colored glasses, but the box office results and fandom are hard to ignore. *The Substance* will get close to cracking $50 million at the box office.[74] *Longlegs* cracked $100 million.[75] *Strange Darling* ran a campaign that was almost all word of mouth and while it had modest box office success, it is making more on VOD rentals and is almost guaranteed to become a cult favorite. Audiences are paying attention, and even mainstream audiences are starting to pay attention to all of the great stuff that is released outside of the Hollywood system. In turn, I am hoping that it starts to turn some people on to older movies that wouldn't be algorithm friendly. If you enjoy *The Substance*, I hope it opens up the world of David Cronenberg and body horror to you. Maybe movies like *Society* or *The Brood* or newer stuff like *Titane* and *Possessor* will get more attention. If you enjoy *Longlegs*, there are so many great serial killer thrillers above and beyond the most popular ones (*Silence of the Lambs*), like *Fallen* or *Manhunter* or *Cure* or *Watcher*.

Unfortunately, even with this trend making me feel better about the state of indie movies, the biggest players in the market are still looking for home runs with the most mass appeal. They are risk-averse, as Cord Jefferson said, even to their detriment, and that is why you probably

74   Esita Mallik, "*The Substance* Box Office (Worldwide): Demi Moore's Film Crosses the $50M Milestone!," Koimoi, November 18, 2024, koimoi.com/box-office/the-substance-box-office-worldwide-demi-moores-film-crosses-the-50m-milestone.

75   "Neon's *Longlegs* Crosses $100 Million to Become Highest-Grossing Indie of 2024," TheWrap, August 16, 2024, thewrap.com/longlegs-box-office-records-neon.

feel like they aren't making movies "for you" anymore. They aren't. You're right. They are making movies for shareholders and to pump up their executive bonuses. But I don't want to hold them all equal in this criticism, because they aren't.

The two worst offenders of this cookie-cutter, risk-averse mentality are Warner Brothers and Disney, and it is no surprise that while they have had many successes, they also took some of the worst losses in recent movie history. It is also no surprise that I would view them as the two most "corporate" studios (Universal is a close third) with leadership that has no interest in the arts. They are led purely by business executives who focus on acquisitions and profit over producing good content with exciting creative direction. If good content leads to more money, they will be happy, but they are equally as happy if the most mainstream vanilla content lands them the same result. They are becoming boring and predictable in a way that is killing the industry, in my opinion. To give you a clear picture of what I am talking about, we only have to look as far as the current leadership behind each of the Big Five studios and the backgrounds that led them to their current roles.

At Disney, Bob Iger is back in charge after a couple of years off. Iger is a corporate executive who has been in leadership roles with ABC and Disney since the mid-'80s. He was never a creative type, and although he worked on some television productions, he has always been a businessman first. He has been wildly successful in that role, acquiring Pixar, Marvel Studios, Lucasfilm, and 20th Century Fox during his tenure across different leadership roles. From a strictly business standpoint, he was nailing what Disney wanted. He was growing the business through acquisitions and keeping shareholders happy.

However, over the past several years I would argue that Disney has slipped when it comes to the big IPs that they rely on for all of their financial success. They have gone all-in on Marvel and Disney limited series on Disney+, and although they had early success with shows like *The Mandalorian* and *WandaVision*, they have fallen off since then. Shows like *The Acolyte* and *The Book of Boba Fett* could not make it past one season, while even *The Mandalorian* has lost most of the hype that surrounded the first two seasons. Marvel projects like *She-Hulk*, *Echo*, *Secret Invasion*, and *Agatha All Along* have almost no buzz compared to the hype that surrounded *WandaVision* and *Loki*. As a result, Marvel movies have also struggled to recapture the magic since the release of *The Avengers: Endgame*. They got greedy, oversaturated the market, and turned away even the most hardcore fans like myself.

The innovation and original storytelling that originally drove these franchises has been replaced with convoluted, interconnected, and boring timelines that leave viewers wanting for the simpler days of Luke Skywalker versus Darth Vader and Thanos versus The Avengers. Iger has admitted to the recent failure and has vowed to cut back on the Marvel and *Star Wars* content—but what will replace it? Original storytelling, or another acquisition that they can run into the ground?

On the Warner Brothers side, the man in charge is David Zaslav. If you follow the industry, Zaslav is widely considered to be one of the worst and most out of touch executives in Hollywood when it comes to the protection of the arts. Zaslav is a former lawyer turned media executive who is responsible for the Discovery Channel's shift from educational programming to reality TV shows. As far back as 2008, he was quoted as saying that he wanted Discovery to be "no longer a cable company, [but] a content company."[76] He was ahead of the times when it came to the changes at Discovery and their shift toward digital media and new forms of entertainment, and he probably would have been a successful executive if he had stayed in that lane. Unfortunately for film fans, when

76   David Goetzl, "Zaslav Holds to Growth Plan at Discovery," MediaPost, April 24, 2008, mediapost.com/publications/article/81311/zaslav-holds-to-growth-plan-at-discovery.html.

Discovery and Warner Media merged in 2022, Zaslav took the helm, and he applied the same mindset to the film industry.

Warner Brothers had a disastrous string of failures in the DC Comics world with *The Flash* and *Joker: Folie à Deux*, lost Christopher Nolan and his original storytelling to Universal, and went all-in on streaming with Max, essentially killing the HBO brand and name recognition. Now, Warner has shifted their focus to a new Batman universe with Robert Pattinson and Colin Farrell's Penguin leading the way, as well as expanding the IPs of *Dune*, Godzilla/Kong, *Game of Thrones*, and Harry Potter. They are all-in on IPs, just like Disney, and they have essentially abandoned support for original films. It is no surprise Christopher Nolan took his talents elsewhere.

Zaslav has also notoriously canceled film projects late into production, like *Batgirl* and *Coyote vs. Acme*. While neither may have been hits, it is beyond cruel to have a team of filmmakers and actors and talented creatives work for years on a film, essentially finish the film, and then pull out the rug from underneath them at the last minute for tax breaks. The worst he could do for them is to release the films to Max, but he is more concerned about money. When the focus shifts from movies and the theatrical experience to streaming services like Max that are losing hundreds of millions of dollars each year,[77] you have to make that up somewhere. It sucks, because almost all of the studio-led services are losing this kind of money, and their only play is desperation, milking their famous IPs for everything they have to try and attract new subscribers. Zaslav wants to keep his job and his $50 million annual compensation package,[78] so he will do whatever it takes to please the board and the shareholders. Art and creativity get in the way of that.

Contrast Iger and Zaslav to someone like Brian Robbins, the current president and CEO of Paramount Pictures who started the role in 2021. Robbins is an actor, writer, producer, and director who has worked in the film industry since the early 1980s. Robbins directed one of my all-time favorite films as a kid, *Good Burger* (it still holds up as one of the funniest kid-friendly comedies ever made), and directed *Varsity Blues*, *Hardball*, and *The Perfect Score*. Robbins is also responsible for the creation of the Nickelodeon show *All That* and was an executive producer on popular shows like *Smallville* and *One Tree Hill*. He has an extensive resume across all kinds of different

77   Rebecca Rubin, "Max Hits 103 Million Subscribers as WBD Reports Earnings," IndieWire, April 25, 2024, indiewire.com/news/business/max-hbo-103-million-subscribers-wbd-earnings-1235033424.

78   Mark Mwachiro, "Warner Bros. Discovery CEO David Zaslav Receives $51.9 Million Pay Package for 2024," *Adweek*, April 11, 2025, adweek.com/tvnewser/david-zaslav-cnn-wbd-pay-package-51-million.

roles in Hollywood, truly a product of the industry and someone who loves film and entertainment. He is the type of person I would pick to run a studio, and from what I have heard in the industry, he is well-respected and well-liked by the creatives he works with.

Robbins has had decent success in his role running Paramount Pictures, with numerous hits under his belt from both IPs and original stories. He smartly evaluated movies like *Smile* and *Mean Girls* (the 2024 musical version) and moved them from direct-to-streaming releases into the theatrical market. *Smile* made over $200 million as an original horror movie which has already spawned a successful sequel that has grossed over $125 million.[79] *Mean Girls* grossed over $100 million and dominated the box office during a slow January in 2024.[80] Those movies could have both been dumped on Paramount+ to try and drive more subscribers to the service, but Robbins understood the value of the theatrical experience and saw the potential for both titles and hit the mark.

However, as rosy as all that sounds, even Robbins is taking the same path that Iger and Zaslav are taking. In a *Variety* article from 2023, Robbins was quoted as saying, "We're

79   Brennan Klein, "*Smile* Box Office Passes $200M and Is 2022's Highest Grossing Horror Film," *Screen Rant*, November 6, 2022, screenrant.com/smile-movie-box-office-update-horror-2022-comparison.

80   "*Mean Girls* (2024)," Box Office Mojo, boxofficemojo.com/title/tt11762114.

not going to release an expensive original animated movie and just pray people will come."[81] Robbins has also shifted focus to key IPs at Paramount when it comes to animation, like *SpongeBob SquarePants*, *Paw Patrol*, and *Teenage Mutant Ninja Turtles*, and live action, like *Mission: Impossible*, *Scream*, *A Quiet Place*, *Top Gun*, and *Gladiator*. Regardless of the shift, Paramount has experienced heavy business losses and layoffs, and I am sure that if push comes to shove, Robbins will be protecting his salary and bonuses just like the rest of them.

These aren't necessarily bad guys or villains. They are executives being paid a ton of money to run big companies and make other rich people even richer. They are capitalists, first and foremost. When money matters more than art, that is when it all starts to fall apart. I still have hope because there are good projects released or distributed by the Big Five and their independent arms, like Searchlight Pictures (Disney), Sony Pictures Classics, Blumhouse (Universal), Miramax (Paramount), and of course, Lionsgate, MGM (Amazon), NEON, A24, Annapurna, and many others. But if the lawyer (Zaslav), business executive (Iger), and creative talent (Robbins) are all in the same boat when it comes to their studios,

81   Brent Lang, "After a Decade in Limbo, Brian Robbins Is Giving Paramount a Makeover with *Ninja Turtles*, Tom Cruise and *Gladiator 2*," *Variety*, July 26, 2023, variety.com/2023/film/features/brian-robbins-paramount-pictures-tmnt-mutant-mayhem-tom-cruise-1235679142.

then what is going wrong? It looks like a vicious cycle that we are in the middle of right now.

Original films were not getting audiences to the theater and driving excitement, so they focused on IPs and remakes, sequels, and reboots. That was successful for a time, and they made money. But in the case of Disney, that well has already started to dry up, and I am sure Warner and Paramount are only just behind them there. So where do they go from there? Back to original storytelling? Audiences seemingly won't show up for those, because of the way they consume media these days. When you live in a bubble curated by social media algorithms, you keep getting the same content you are comfortable with. New and original ideas are sometimes uncomfortable, and therefore, are risky bets. No executive living on a comfy multi-million-dollar salary wants to lose their job on a risky bet. At least if the franchise movie bombs, they can blame the filmmakers or the marketing team. For an original idea that they greenlit, they would be scrutinized far more.

So how do we all break out of this vicious cycle? How do we get back to the "golden ages" of Hollywood, where original ideas first originated? Because there is no *Star Wars* franchise without *Star Wars*. There is no *Halloween* (2018) without *Halloween* (1978). Even more recently, there is no *A Quiet Place: Day One* without the incredible original film. Taking it a step further, there would be no *Star Wars* without *2001: A Space Odyssey*, and no movies like *Longlegs* without *Silence of the Lambs* or *Se7en*. Even if they did not spawn a franchise full of sequels, hundreds of original, standalone films inspired today's filmmakers, and hundreds of films inspired the filmmakers who inspired them, going back over a hundred years. To lose that means we lose the future of movies. It means that the next Martin Scorsese or Quentin Tarantino will be directing *Star Wars: Episode XIX* or *Dune: Part Seven* instead of something new and fresh, because that is what they grew up on. So, how do we break the vicious cycle? We need to break free from the algorithm, so here is how to do it.

PART 3

HOW TO WATCH MOVIES OUTSIDE OF THE ALGORITHM & ADAPT TO THE FUTURE

You've now read a hundred pages of slightly depressing writing about how movies have changed forever and are currently going through some serious growing pains as the industry and filmmakers try to adapt to the new landscape of film. I apologize if it seemed gloomy, but it was important to ground everyone in where we all stand right now as consumers and audiences to understand how we can all make small shifts that allow us to break free from this system and the algorithms. There is still a way to support smaller movies and movie theaters and build some grassroots momentum as a huge community of dedicated film enthusiasts to celebrate art in an increasingly capitalistic world.

As viewing habits have shifted and people have settled into their entertainment "bubbles," a major problem I have noticed is a serious lack of discoverability of new films. When I say "new," I don't just mean the latest releases, but things that would be new to you. If you were born in 1992, like me, then you have decades of films that were released before you existed. There are hundreds of incredible movies from this time that deserve to be seen. Who knows, maybe your favorite movie ends up being from the 1960s. Maybe you find a filmmaker from the 1950s who inspired another filmmaker from the 1980s who in turn inspired your favorite modern-day filmmaker. You may go down a rabbit hole of movies that ends up shaping your interests as you grow up.

As I mentioned in my introduction, my twenties were as influential to my interests in film as anything from my childhood, and I am afraid that younger generations will not have this same experience. People born in the 2000s or 2010s have grown up in a world where video stores don't exist. Streaming is the first option for watching movies. They are locked into the algorithm because the world around them adapted without their permission or influence. They were not given a say in the matter, and now they are not given a say in what is presented to them as entertainment.

If you think I am exaggerating, put down this book for a moment and open Netflix or Max or Hulu. Look at what is recommended to you. The front page of your Netflix interface will be 90 percent Netflix Originals with the red "N" in the top right corner. Max will be full of the Warner Brothers/Discovery IPs and Max Originals. Hulu will be more of the same, with original content pushed to the forefront and Disney or 20th Century Fox titles surrounding them.

Do you see any older movies? Any classics that aren't tied to some modern remake, sequel, or television series? My guess would be that you don't, and that is a real problem because by pushing only the latest original content, the major streaming services are essentially erasing decades of film history from the modern consciousness. I think about thrillers like *The Night of the Hunter* or *The Friends of Eddie Coyle*. I think about horror movies like *Alice Sweet Alice* and *Don't Look Now,* or a personal favorite, *The Sentinel.* Comedies like *Moonstruck* and *I Wanna Hold Your Hand.*

One of my favorite movies I have seen recently is *After Hours*, a nightmarish black comedy with one of the best depictions of 1980s New York City ever put to screen. It is a film that will leave you guessing until the end, and one of the most surreal movies I have ever seen. It is also directed by Martin Scorsese, which might shock some people who think they know all of Scorsese's movies. You wouldn't be alone—this is one of his lesser-known gems, and you would be hard-pressed to see it recommended on any major streaming platform. If you haven't seen it, I highly recommend it, and it is a great example of the type of film that can get lost under the weight of the more popular *Goodfellas* and *Wolf of Wall Street* types that dominate the public consciousness.

Using *After Hours* as an example, I went looking for where it is streaming and found that it is only available on Prime Video. Being a longtime Prime member and user of their video streaming app, I was curious if *After Hours* would appear on a recommendation list, as it is exactly the kind of movie I like. I had not watched it on Prime Video yet (I watched the incredible 4K UHD disc from The Criterion Collection), so it would have made sense for it to appear in my "Movies We Think You'll Like" or "Top Picks for You" feeds. As you probably guessed, it was not among the roughly fifty or sixty movies recommended to me. Backing up my fear of older movies being ignored, the oldest film that was recommended to me was *Death Becomes Her* from 1992. A great film, released the same year I was born. It was almost like they didn't want to go past anything I wasn't alive for.

While Prime did recommend a few movies right up my alley, like the excellent *Red Rooms*, terrifying *Lake Mungo*, and a few other recent picks like *Longlegs*, *A Real Pain*, and *Oddity*, it failed to show me much variety outside of the last two decades. There were a couple of films from the 1990s, but that was as far back as they went with their recommendations. My theory is that they think that older movies won't play with most of their audience because of the pacing and the style of these movies. They probably assume, and possibly rightfully so, that they need to recommend the most recognizable movies in order to keep people interested, hence why even the "older" movies I was served included massive hits like *Good Will Hunting*, *Hook*, *LA Confidential*, and *The Sandlot*.

I don't think that any of this is malicious, but the algorithms running these services know that they are competing for attention with social media and the rest of the internet. If it isn't a trending topic or something new and fresh, it will get overlooked by the user in favor of another entertainment channel. They have a business to run, and their business is your eyes on their apps. They push what they know will get them clicks and engagement, watch hours, and time spent on the app. These are the success metrics that run modern Hollywood.

Luckily, there is a simple solution if you want to build your own "Netflix" at home and explore decades of films that aren't on the streaming apps. That wonderful solution is good ol' physical media. DVDs, Blu-rays, VHS, Laserdiscs—it doesn't matter which format you choose. But I think you will be shocked at how many movies are unavailable on streaming and video-on-demand services compared to physical media. Even better, if you approach building your collection smartly, you might even save a few bucks on your media spending by dropping a few streaming services.

According to the Deloitte 2024 Digital Media Trends Report, the average US household spends $61 per month on streaming services with subscriptions to four different platforms.[82] That number has steadily increased each year as the platforms have fragmented over the last decade and the costs to maintain a user base have increased significantly. We are a long way from the days of Netflix, Hulu, HBO Go, and Prime Video being the only options. In those days, each service offered a ton of titles from major studios like Disney, Paramount, Warner Brothers, Lionsgate, and Universal, as well as a fair share of indie productions.

These days, every platform is focused on their original programming as most of the studios have taken on the development of their own streaming platforms. Now, we have Apple TV+, Disney+, Paramount+, Peacock, Max, MGM+, AMC+—the list goes on and on. It is no wonder that most households have four streaming subscriptions because of all of the different available options. It harkens back to the old days of cable TV packages that would include add-ons like Cinemax, HBO, Showtime, and Starz.

82   China Widener et al., "2025 Digital Media Trends: Social Platforms Are Becoming a Dominant Force in Media and Entertainment," Deloitte Center for Technology, Media & Telecommunications, March 25, 2025, www2.deloitte.com/us/en/insights/industry/technology/digital-media-trends-consumption-habits-survey.html.

Basically, streaming has become cable 2.0, and people are paying the price for that access.

As the competitive landscape for streaming grew, so did the budgets that each service needed to create original content. I remember the days when a show like *Stranger Things* was a novelty, or when Netflix first won Emmy awards and people were questioning if they were actually "television." Now, it is all so second nature, and the spending has grown to levels that are putting the customers on the hook for more money. I will cover the changes that have taken place in Hollywood and the craziness of streaming originals later, but if Netflix and Disney want to spend hundreds of millions of dollars on original content, someone needs to pay for it. And that someone is the general public.

Since 2022, Netflix has raised their ad-free prices each year by $2–$3 per month depending on the plan. As of their latest increase in January 2025, Netflix premium with 4K content now costs $24.99/month, up from $11.99/month in 2013.[83] The ad-free version of Hulu has gone from $12.99 in 2022 to $18.99 in 2024.[84] Max has been less dramatic, raising its prices by just $1 each year in

83   Troy Reeder, "Netflix Pricing History," 9meters, January 22, 2025, 9meters.com/entertainment/streaming/netflix-pricing-history.

84   "Hulu Plans and Prices," Hulu Help Center, help.hulu.com/article/hulu-how-much-does-hulu-cost.

2023 and 2024.[85] Paramount+ also joined in the price increases, raising their prices by a couple of dollars over the last several years.[86] This is all to be expected, as continuous growth needs for shareholders, increased spend on original content and licensing, and inflation have all driven the costs of running these services up. Yay, capitalism!

But they all pale in comparison to the biggest offender, Disney. Disney+ has gone from an annual cost of $75 at launch in 2021 to double that in 2024 with an annual cost of $150, and more price increases to come.[87] I understand capitalism and inflation, and the years between 2020 and 2024 have been volatile and expensive. Everything costs more. But Disney+ going through a 100 percent price increase over three years has much more to do with corporate greed, poor financial decisions, and overspending on saturated content than it does economic conditions. Conveniently enough, at the same time that Disney has increased their streaming prices two-fold,

85   Emma Roth, "Max Raises Prices Across Its Ad-Free Plans," *The Verge*, June 4, 2024, theverge.com/2024/6/4/24171193/max-price-raise-ad-free-plans-hbo.

86   Malcolm McMillan, "Paramount Plus Price Hike Is Official: What You'll Pay Now and How to Get Around It," Tom's Guide, August 22, 2024, tomsguide.com/entertainment/streaming/paramount-plus-price-hike-is-official-what-youll-pay-now-and-how-to-get-around-it.

87   Charles Pulliam-Moore, "The Price of Disney Plus Is About to Go Up," *The Verge*, August 6, 2024, theverge.com/2024/8/6/24214550/disney-plus-espn-and-hulu-october-price-hike.

they have also significantly shrunk their investment in physical media, stripping it completely from regions like Australia, closing down the popular Disney Movie Club that supplied many collectors with physical copies of Disney releases, and occasionally outright ignoring major releases like *Barbarian*, a surprise hit horror movie that grossed over $45 million at the box office in 2022[88] and has yet to see an official physical media release as of early 2025.

To their credit, Disney has made an attempt to bring some of this back more recently, partnering with Sony on a physical media distribution deal in North America over the summer of 2024 to get more titles out to the market, including some Disney+ shows like *The Mandalorian* and *WandaVision* that were previously locked on the streaming service. However, much like Netflix only licensing out major titles like *The Irishman* to labels like The Criterion Collection, it all comes down to money. Hundreds of shows and movies on various streaming services will never see the light of day in a physical media format.

If we think about the cost, and the ever-increasing hit to your wallet from streaming services, an argument can be made that physical media may be cheaper in

88   *"Barbarian,"* Box Office Mojo, boxofficemojo.com/title/tt15791034.

the long-term based on the average person's viewing habits. According to a survey conducted in 2022 by Plex, a global streaming/media server company, and OnePoll, the average American has thirteen movies on their watchlists.[89] That seems like a fair number; it means that, like me, many people have a backlog of movies they want to watch but simply have not had the time for yet. Another survey conducted during the summer of 2020, during what I would consider to be the peak of streaming due to COVID-19 restrictions, found that the average American was watching ten movies per month.[90] I would assume that this number has since fallen, but for the purposes of my argument, let's stick with ten movies per month as a baseline. If we use an estimated cost of $5 per movie, assuming that you are buying DVD or Blu-ray, the two most popular formats, the average cost of watching ten movies per month would be $50. As I previously noted, the most recent studies from 2023 had the average American spending $61 per month on streaming services. If you want to watch ten movies per month, I would argue that physical media is cheaper.

89   "New Study Finds Half of Americans Struggle to Find Where to Watch Streaming Content," PR Newswire, September 13, 2022, prnewswire.com/news-releases/new-study-finds-half-of-americans-struggle-to-find-where-to-watch-streaming-content-301622418.html.

90   "The Average American Watched at Least 20 Movies This Summer, Study Says," *People*, September 30, 2020, people.com/movies/the-average-american-watched-at-least-20-movies-this-summer.

There is also a cost savings because of the different sales models used by physical media and streaming services. When you invest in physical media, there is a one-time cost to owning a movie. You pay $5 for a Blu-ray, and you watch that as many times as you like. This is the typical retail sales model that we are all used to working with. However, with streaming, the goal is to get subscriptions and recurring revenue. You pay $15 per month, and you do that until you take the action to cancel the subscription. This is essentially the SaaS (software as a service) sales model, and its goal is consistent revenue with growth driven by price hikes and subscriber increases. Ideally, more subscribers would mean fewer price increases, but many times, like in the case of Netflix's price increase in 2025 after seeing a record-breaking nineteen million new subscribers in Q4 of 2024,[91] companies will pull both levers to increase their stock value. Streaming services have fully adopted this model and made many changes over the past few years that clearly show that they are striving to be successful software services and growth machines first, and entertainment providers second.

The SaaS model has been popularized over the last ten years by major enterprise software companies like

---

91   Wendy Lee, "Netflix Had a Record-Breaking Quarter. Here Come the Price Hikes," *Los Angeles Times*, January 21, 2025, latimes.com/entertainment-arts/business/story/2025-01-21/netflix-releases-fourth-quarter-earnings-results.

Adobe, Microsoft, Salesforce, Google, Amazon, and Shopify. Many companies like Adobe and Microsoft used to offer their products for one-time purchases, using licenses to attach the software to specific computers. For example, you could buy a license to Microsoft Office (Word, PowerPoint, Excel) for $99. This gave you lifetime access to the tool on one computer for as long as you owned the device. Adobe would do the same thing with their creative tools like Photoshop and Premiere Pro.

These companies realized that it is hard to keep growing revenue when a one-time purchase is the biggest driver of sales. As technology improved and people were upgrading their equipment and software less often, the sales of lifetime licenses dipped. In a world driven by capitalism and shareholders, that wasn't going to fly. So, they made the shift from a $99 lifetime license downloaded to a device to a $9.99 per month subscription hosted in the cloud. Now, a customer who sticks with them for five years is worth over $500 instead of $99. There are additional costs to hosting all of this software in the cloud, but those are outweighed by the constant stream of new revenue. No wonder they are some of the biggest companies in the world!

They also realized that once you have cornered the market and have your users locked, you can do whatever you want with pricing. You might lose a few customers if you raise the price, but you can raise it whenever you want. A simple math equation will tell these companies that while they can expect to lose 5 percent of their customers after a price hike, they will gain more than they lose by increasing the price. $9.99 per month can easily become $12.99, $15.99, or $19.99 over the course of a few years. Best of all, you are still locked to a single device unless you want to pay more for additional licenses for extra monthly costs. Does this sound familiar?

Streaming services have adopted many of the same techniques as SaaS companies when it comes to their business practices, pricing, and sales model. This is why I would refer to them as SaaS companies at this point. They host a cloud-based software service that charges a monthly subscription fee. Whether you are word processing, editing a photo, or watching a movie, it is all the same on the backend.

The major streaming services have also started to crack down on password sharing, which is one of the major cons of running a SaaS business. Every software company deals with it, but much like locking down a license to a specific device, streaming services have now started locking down their entertainment to specific IP addresses and locations or offering more expensive family plans.

You might be able to get away with sharing a password with a neighbor if you live in the same building, but it is likely that all of the major services will crack down on password sharing now that subscription rates have slowed from their peak.

They didn't have a problem with sharing the service when they were signing up record-breaking amounts of users each month. In fact, they probably encouraged it. It got people addicted to the service and hooked them on the shows and movies. Now they can pull the rug out from under those people and hope that their need for the latest trending movie or show will get them to sign up for their own plan. It's a perfect plan, and I am sure it will work.

But this again brings up another cost benefit to physical media versus streaming. Physical media is a flat fee. It is the old Microsoft Office model. $5 for a disc, and you own it forever. In fact, it's even better, because it isn't locked down to a specific device. You can share it with a friend, watch it at your parents' house, and if you end up not liking the movie, you have an asset that you can use to get a few bucks back. It isn't an investment, and nobody should buy Blu-rays expecting to make money on them. But if you do spend $20 on a new release and end up not liking it, it would be easy to flip that online for $10–$15 and get some of your money back.

You are in total control of your spending as well, so you only need to buy what you want to watch. If you want to spend $100 on movies in a month, you can do that. If you need to cut back one month, you can spend nothing. You set your budget and your monthly costs instead of being at the mercy of a corporation out to make as much money as they can. Some months you might spend a lot on movies, and some months you might not. But if the average annual cost of streaming is $732 ($61 per month for twelve months), you can buy a hell of a lot of movies for less than that if you are a smart shopper.

Looking out even longer term, it is inevitable that streaming prices will continue to increase. If you told me that in five years the average American household would spend over $100 per month on streaming, I would not be surprised. At the same time, although prices for new-release physical media are rising due to increased manufacturing costs and a shrinking market, the cost of buying used media is lower than ever and will continue to shrink as more used media enters the market. People ditched their DVDs and Blu-rays for streaming, and now lots can be found online for pennies on the dollar, or even free, on eBay, Facebook Marketplace, and other seller sites. If you go to a flea market or pawn shop, you will find tons of movies for cheap prices.

There isn't a ton of competition for used physical media, so the prices keep dropping as retail stores and people cleaning out their homes just want to get rid of their collections. One person's trash is another person's treasure, right? Take advantage of it now while it is still good, because I do think there will be a resurgence of people wanting to buy back their DVDs and Blu-rays as streaming continues to expand. Cost is one reason, but the other reason for a resurgence will be the availability, or the lack thereof, of so many movies and TV shows on current platforms.

As we know from the meticulous work of Ralph Tribbey from the DVD and Blu-ray Release Report, if we combine the DVD, Blu-ray, and 4K UHD formats together, there are around 400,000 official releases available on the market.[92] If VHS tapes were included, although there are no official numbers available, I would guess that there are tens, if not hundreds, of thousands more movies that never made it to even the DVD format. In the interest of this argument, I want to get even more specific with the numbers, so I dove into the DVD & Blu-ray Release Report

92   Ralph Tribbey, "DVD & Blu-ray Release Report," dvdandblurayreleasereport. com.

Lost in the Stream

again to see how many of these hundreds of thousands of releases were actually movies versus special-interest releases, TV shows, or other miscellaneous forms of media. After breaking it down, I came up with a total of 179,062 movies in the three formats. Knowing that there is overlap between the formats, I believe that 150,000 movies is a fair number to work with as of 2024. Just to show I am not biased, I can align this number with my friends at Scarecrow Video, the largest video store and video collection in the world, who have 147,000 titles (and counting) in their collection.[93]

Of course, the big question is, how many of these movies are worth watching? And how could you possibly watch them all? At an average of two hours per movie, 150,000 movies would take over thirty-four years to watch. However, I think everyone who made the movies would say that their movie is worth watching for one reason or another, and not every movie is made for every person. The beauty is that there is something for everyone, and you can pick and choose from all of these movies. Movies are art, and I am certainly not one to judge why someone creates or enjoys art. I have my tastes and criticisms, and I have no interest in seeing all 150,000 of these movies. All I know is that they should be protected, as other forms of art are. With so many different tastes

93   "Our Story," Scarecrow Video, scarecrowvideo.org/our-story.

and interests in the world of film, I am sure that many of them have an audience that would enjoy them. There are a lot of deep cuts, essentially unknown indie films, tons of international films, and lots of smaller projects that you've probably never heard of. But someone will want to watch them, and the fact that they are accessible and not lost forever is a good thing for the art form of movies.

Now, prepare to be shocked. Here are the same numbers from the most popular streaming services as of October 2023:[94]

- Amazon Prime: 12,071 movies
- Netflix: 3,977 movies
- Peacock: 3,950 movies
- Hulu: 2,419 movies
- Max: 2,168 movies
- Disney+: 1,400 movies
- Paramount+: 830 movies

If we total all of those up, ignoring any overlap, there are 26,815 movies available on the major streaming services—less than 18 percent of the total movies available on DVD and Blu-ray. Since most people are paying for an average

94   Julia Stoll, "Number of Domestic Movies Released on Video Streaming Services in the United States from 2021 to 2023," Statista, March 19, 2025, statista.com/statistics/1459967/number-movies-selected-streaming-services-us.

Lost in the Stream

of four services, it is likely that the average person has access to 20,000 movies, and that number is far less if they are not subscribed to Amazon Prime, which has the largest catalog by far.

Other smaller streamers like The Criterion Channel (roughly 2,500 movies), Shudder (600–700 movies), and Mubi (800 movies) also have a decent catalog, as well as free platforms like Hoopla and Kanopy (a personal favorite—free streaming and no ads!) that have thousands of more movies depending on your location. There are also ad-supported streamers like Roku and Tubi that have tens of thousands of movies and TV shows. It was hard to find an exact number of movies, as these free services have an even higher fluctuation in available titles than the paid services, but based on my knowledge of both platforms, a lot of their titles are TV shows, and it is unclear how they count titles. Some services count a single season of TV as one title, while others count the whole show as one title—but I would guess that when everyone is fighting over numbers, each season, and possibly each episode, of a show counts as a "title."

Outside of streaming, digital rentals and digital purchases can be made on most devices. Fandango at Home (formerly VUDU), the world's largest video-on-demand rental platform, boasts a catalog of over 250,000 movies and TV shows.[95] However, after looking at their platform, I noticed that they sell individual TV episodes. You can buy season one of *Friends*, but you can also buy just episodes three, seven, and twelve. I would bet that they are counting each episode as a "title," so that 250,000 number is highly inflated when you consider how many thousands of individual TV episodes are out there. It is hard to get an accurate number on how many movies are on Fandango at Home, but I can use Amazon Prime Video's rental service as a good estimate, which has "over 60,000 movies" available to rent. I would put Fandango at Home higher than that, but a fair estimate is probably 70,000 to 80,000 movies. Either way, it is still significantly less than what is available on DVD and Blu-ray.

Finally, the biggest reason I prefer physical media to streaming, although I do use both, is how it helps me discover new movies and make intentional selections when I pick what to watch. When my wife and I have a few free hours at night after the kids go to bed, we will often watch either a movie, a comedy show (*Veep* and *Detroiters* are two recent favorites), or a true crime documentary. Those are pretty much our three rotations, and depending on how we are feeling and how tired we are, we will switch it up every day. When we have the

95 "Discover," Fandango at Home, athome.fandango.com/content/movies/discover.

energy and the motivation for a movie, it almost always comes straight from my collection for a few reasons.

First, I have curated this collection of movies over many years. It reflects my tastes and interests. So, when I browse those shelves, I am not going through the latest recommendations or "what's trending" on a service. I am looking through movies from all sorts of genres and time periods, taking the time to pull some options off the shelf, read the synopsis, examine the artwork, and hold the case in my hand. It may sound strange, but there is something different about holding the physical copy of a movie and making a connection with it. It becomes more meaningful and less of a throwaway option to fill the time. That's where the other options come into play.

If we are tired, or aren't in the mood for a movie, the response from one of us will often be something like, "Ugh, let's just watch *Veep*." And that isn't a slight against *Veep*, or *The Office*, or *Detroiters*, or one of our favorite true crime programs, *Forensic Files*. We love all of those shows dearly and they have talented people behind them. My wife and I have seen every episode of all of them multiple times. But there is a difference between "throwing something on the TV" and "watching something." That is the difference between scrolling through an app for something to "put on" and choosing a movie off a shelf, putting it in the player, investing time, and giving all of your focus to that movie.

If you think back to your childhood and the nostalgic memories that you have of your favorite movies, a lot of that is probably tied to either a theatrical experience, or an experience with a home video release. You remember the artwork on the case from your favorite VHS tape or DVD. You remember rewinding the tape after each watch, the interactive DVD menu, or the special features that were included. You remember the theater you saw the movie at and who you went to see the movie with. A lot of us probably kept ticket stubs as a souvenir—I know I did. We all had this special connection to a physical item or a time and place, which simply does not happen when you sit on the couch and flip through Netflix to see what's new. That special feeling missing is another reason why sometimes modern Hollywood films can feel like throwaway content—it's because they know who's watching, and they are catering to that. They are making throwaway content for disinterested audiences.

If you haven't already, give physical media some more thought. Start a small collection of your favorite movies, or buy some cheap copies of movies you think you would enjoy and make the calculated decision to watch them with full focus. Buy what you love, or what you think you might love, and don't just go out and start buying all of the latest and greatest limited editions if you can't afford it. Start with the basics and branch out from there.

My movie collection started with Denzel Washington movies and a few of the big mainstream classics like *Jaws*, *Halloween*, *Jurassic Park*, and *Back to the Future*. Then I branched out from there as I found similar movies or discovered new physical media labels that were releasing tons of hidden gems and cult classics. I stumbled upon The Criterion Collection and their collection of classic films because I loved David Fincher films, I wanted to watch *The Game* (an incredible film if you have never seen it), and The Criterion Collection was the only way to own it on DVD or Blu-ray. I found Scream Factory and their lineup of cult horror classics and '80s slashers because I wanted to own *Halloween II* and *Halloween III*, and they were the only ones who had released it on Blu-ray. I discovered Kino Lorber because they were the only ones who had released *Nosferatu* and *The Cabinet of Dr. Caligari*, and I wanted to get into more films like that to explore the origins of horror movies. I now own hundreds of films from these labels, and so many more amazing independent labels like Vinegar Syndrome, Arrow Video, and Umbrella Entertainment. Many of them would not be sitting in my collection or have come across my radar at all if it wasn't for my interest in physical media and the expansion of my collection.

All that being said, the negative side to physical media also has to be considered. I would not be an impartial reporter and writer if I did not cover some of that. For one, physical media does create a lot of waste and clutter. Physical media requires plastic cases, discs to be manufactured, and lots of shipping time and packaging. There are arguments as to what is more environmentally friendly—streaming and emissions from data centers or physical media manufacturing—but nobody can deny that physical media does introduce plastic into the world. It pales in comparison to other things like clothing and electronics, but it does contribute to mass consumerism and waste, drowning the world in plastic.

It also takes up a ton of space and can easily start to build up around your house. For people who struggle with clutter or hoarding, buying physical media and starting a new collection would probably be a net negative for you. With any sort of addictive personality or hoarding mentality, any of the cost arguments I threw out versus streaming would all be for nothing. I have seen people online go broke and deep into debt from buying movies. That is not worth it, and it never will be. If that sounds like an issue for you, stick with the streaming services.

They give you a flat rate each month and less impulsive buying or FOMO (fear of missing out) purchases just because you saw someone else buy something online. I have been there myself and had to reel it back in.

If all of that sounds too overwhelming or scary, other forms of "physical media" are currently available or coming to the market that resolve some of those problems. I think that optical discs are probably on their way out in the next decade for several of the reasons above, plus the lack of sales growth and increasing cost of manufacturing movies. In their place, I envision physical media becoming reliant on hard drives and different forms of media storage. This helps to solve the issue of waste, keeps the costs for restorations and home video releases down, and still allows you, the consumer, to physically own the movies. Companies like Kaleidescape are already doing this, offering high-quality downloads to their media players that are equal to the Blu-ray and 4K UHD experience you get on a disc.

The differentiator is on-premise storage versus cloud storage. You will own the movies and they are downloaded to your own hard drive, which in my eyes, gives you the same level of ownership that a disc does. If something sits in the cloud or on a streaming service, it can be taken away. If it is downloaded to a hard drive, it is yours, and can be transferred to future storage devices. If storage costs continue to drop dramatically, I think that these types of devices are the next frontier for physical media and high-quality playback that hardcore enthusiasts want.

Ultimately, whether you watch a movie on a VHS tape, a Laserdisc, a DVD, a Blu-ray, 4K discs, or off a hard drive, watching a movie on a high-quality physical media format will mean more memorable movie nights and less mindless scrolling of disposable content. Make an effort to rediscover physical media as an extension of your love for film, and you will be happy that you did. But don't just take my word for it. Listen to some of the world's greatest filmmakers, like Martin Scorsese, Quentin Tarantino, Christopher Nolan, Guillermo Del Toro, or Edgar Wright. They all preach the benefits of physical media and its importance to the industry, its importance for film discovery and exploration, and its influence on them as filmmakers. If it is good enough for them, it is good enough for me, and I could not be happier that I took the leap so many years ago and started building my collection again. It took me back to the days of the video store, the shelf of VHS tapes in my childhood home, and a stronger time for human connection to the arts. Long live physical media!

Now that I have officially sounded like an old man yelling from my soapbox for the last several pages, you probably think I am exactly that. I am out of touch and yelling at the sky because the world isn't the same today as it was when I was growing up. It's the old, tired "back in my day" argument that immediately turns your brain off. I get it. I feel the same way when I hear someone start ranting about music or fashion or sports and how things have changed "for the worse." But that is not what I am all about. Several positives have come from this shift that have me excited for the future of entertainment.

For starters, streaming is not all bad. I may have criticisms of the platforms and the way in which their algorithms and business models work, but it is fair to say that there has never been a time in human history when we have had more convenient entertainment options available to us with just a few clicks. The big streaming services are the main players, but I don't think people realize how many options they have out there. Dozens of niche services have popped up that serve a smaller set of customers but offer some of the most incredible movies. I am thinking of services like The Criterion Channel, Arrow Player, Shudder, Screambox, Mubi, Shout TV, Kino Film Collection, and many more. The options are almost limitless, but they come with a cost.

If you want to save a few dollars, tons of movies and TV shows are available for free on services like PlutoTV, FreeVee, FuboTV, Tubi, Crackle, and Fandango at Home. These services still need to make money, so you will be served ads. And yes, sometimes those ads will come in the middle of a movie, which is a cardinal sin in my book. But at least you have the option! Those looking to save a few bucks in the past would have had to wait until a movie was shown on ABC as their "Movie of the Week" or hit cable channels like TNT or TBS. Either way, you would still sit through commercials, and your options were limited to what the network decided to air. Now, there are thousands of free movies available to watch whenever your heart desires.

Services like Kanopy and Hoopla offer free streaming with a library card or university credentials. These services can be rate-limited per month, but they don't have any ads, and they offer an eclectic, revolving selection of indie films and documentaries, as well as plenty of major catalog studio titles. A library card is free, so these services are free, and they are a great resource that not enough people take advantage of. Kanopy is a personal favorite, and in full disclosure, I do work with their team and I like the people over there. But I work with many streaming services, including Netflix, Hulu, Shudder, Shout Factory TV, as well as many of the physical media labels I talk about in this book. What I enjoy about Kanopy, outside of the free streaming with no ads, is its recommendation engine. Yes, it is an algorithm, but just like anything else, algorithms are not inherently bad. If they are used correctly and in a positive manner, they can be an incredible tool. Kanopy's recommendations are some of the most consistent compared to my personal taste, and they also go farther back into the history of film than most streaming services. Movies from the 1920s through the 1970s are just as prevalent and popular as new releases. It is the best streaming service, maybe right up with The Criterion Channel, in terms of discovering new films and expanding your boundaries beyond what's trending.

Some of these services can get you locked into a bubble, but they are also more widely available and easier to access than ever before. It is hard to complain with the options we have, as long as they are used smartly. There are hundreds of thousands of movies available across streaming services. Unless you lived close to a video store juggernaut like Scarecrow Video, the world's largest video store in Seattle, chances are that your local Blockbuster or mom-and-pop rental store did not have near the number of titles now available online.

In a roundabout way, streaming also had a positive impact, or at least a shift that I find to be an improvement, on physical media as well. Alongside the mainstream push for streaming came an amazing wave of independent labels and small retailers offering high-quality physical media releases on the DVD, Blu-ray, and 4K UHD video formats. When I started my physical media collection in 2013, a ton of big-name movies were available from the major studios. Finding a Disney or Warner Brothers title on DVD or Blu-ray was not hard, and most stores had plenty of copies of the big movies. But what didn't exist were a ton of independent labels releasing more interesting deep cuts on disc. The most well-known at the time was probably The Criterion Collection, which had been around for decades with its curated collection of "important classic and contemporary films." But as streaming took hold and more of the major studios moved away from doing in-house home video releases, there was an explosion in independent companies that collectors and enthusiasts refer to as "boutique labels" doing restoration work and releasing their curated collections of DVD, Blu-ray, and 4K physical media.

This was not a new phenomenon, as the heyday of the VHS tape featured labels like this who licensed titles from major studios and released them on home video. It allowed the studios to focus on theatrical releases and pass on the hard work of transferring film to tapes playable at home to the experts. But as the sales rose and the money behind home video looked better every year, the studios began to take over production. Now, as home video sales shrink every year due to the rise of streaming, the studios are looking back at independent partners to do the heavy lifting on the home video side. Disney ceased production of their home video titles completely in 2024, passing their catalog on to Sony, and other studios like Paramount, Warner Brothers, MG (owned by Amazon), and Lionsgate have been doing a lot more licensing to these boutique labels.

These days, there are far more boutique labels than even in the days of VHS. They may not be household names for everyone, but most hardcore movie fans will know of them because it is likely that they have handled the restoration work or latest physical media release for some incredible cult classics, major catalog blockbusters, and tons of independent films from years past that would have been lost without the work of these labels. Some of the major players include Shout Studios and their Scream Factory sub-label, Arrow Video, Kino Lorber, Vinegar Syndrome, and The Criterion Collection, which is still cranking out quality titles after all these years. These labels have released some incredible restorations, including 4K UHD remasters of classic films like *Serpico*

(Kino), *Carrie* (Scream Factory), *The Warriors* (Arrow Video), *Showgirls* (Vinegar Syndrome), and *Citizen Kane* (Criterion).

Smaller labels like Second Sight Releasing, Umbrella Entertainment, ViaVision Entertainment, TerrorVision, Synapse Films, Severin, and Radiance Films have also been steadily releasing cult classics and genre favorites with some of the most intricate box sets and collector's editions that have ever been available. These sets feature essay books, art cards, props, newly commissioned artwork, posters, and oftentimes several cuts of the film. Without these labels, we would not have beautiful 4K remasters of cult movies like *Suspiria* (Synapse), *The Changeling* (Severin), and *Martin* (Second Sight) available to watch in the highest-quality format ever available on home video. I could go on and on, and I will talk more about the impact that physical media can have on how people discover movies and films and build their own taste, but this is just a small taste of another positive impact that streaming has had on the industry.

Finally, I have to give some credit to the Streaming Revolution for the benefits that it provides to independent filmmakers. Before streaming and digital platforms, it was extremely difficult for independent filmmakers to find an audience and get any sort of distribution for their projects. For every *Halloween* or *Blair Witch* that made millions, a thousand other movies never saw the light of day. At the highest level, independent distributors like A24 and NEON dominate the indie film landscape and elevate many incredible stories to the level of major studio blockbusters. Below that are dozens of distributors like IFC Films, Shudder, Dread, Bleecker Street, Gunpowder and Sky, Magnolia, Cinedigm, and many others doing great work getting smaller films from film festivals onto streaming services and released on physical media. Without a platform like streaming, a lot of these films would not see a fraction of the audience that they can reach today.

This is especially true for documentary filmmakers, who I think always struggled to find an audience and monetize their work. With platforms like Netflix and Max thriving on true crime documentaries and stories about the weird characters and subcultures of the world, there is a bigger platform and more opportunity for documentary filmmakers now than there ever has been. Social media also plays a huge part in this, as places like YouTube and Vimeo give filmmakers a free platform to upload their work and potentially reach millions of viewers.

Streaming has opened doors for many filmmakers. It has provided access to a vast library of content that anyone in the world can enjoy with a few clicks. It has done some good for sure, and even as a staunch supporter of physical media, I always think that a balance is best. Buy some movies on physical media and watch some movies on streaming or digital. No harm, no foul on either option. But what about the theaters? How will they survive, given all the headwinds in the industry? What is their future?

When it comes to movie theaters, they definitely have some work to do. Although theaters have a clear advantage over at-home viewing experiences, the technological experience at many theaters can be inconsistent, and at times, poor. I travel for work to Connecticut a few times a year, and I have the luxury of staying in a nice hotel right around the corner from a twenty-screen AMC theater with both IMAX and Dolby Cinema technology. It is one of the biggest theaters in the area and serves many people in the Hartford area. As you can imagine, when I am on a work trip alone and bored after the day ends, going to the movies by myself sure beats sitting in a hotel room and wasting away watching TikTok videos or scrolling through the cable channels. So, I pretty consistently get out and see a movie each night I am down in Connecticut, which is awesome. What isn't awesome is the differences in quality I have seen within this same theater. Within a few months, I have seen three movies at this theater, all in different formats.

I saw *Civil War* in IMAX, *Smile 2* in Dolby Cinema, and *Terrifier 3* in a standard theater presentation. So far, I am not having much luck, as only the Dolby Cinema truly provided a great experience.

When I was watching *Civil War* in IMAX, it was immediately clear that the bulb in the IMAX projector was struggling. The picture was dim, it flickered, and brightness and contrast went up and down throughout the movie. Having a pretty good knowledge of the technology and what things should look like, I was probably the only person to complain, and they did not take it seriously. They offered a refund, but I wanted to see the movie, so I stuck it out. However, I rewatched it at home when it came out on 4K disc, and as I suspected, this was not an aesthetic choice by the filmmakers. The projector bulb was dying, and either nobody noticed, nobody cared, or it was a combination of the two. I do not blame AMC for this entirely, as IMAX is responsible for all of the equipment in their theaters, but I do blame the theater for not having anyone knowledgeable enough to know it was an issue. I contacted IMAX after the showing and they were unaware of the issue (or so they said) and hopefully the next time I go, the bulb will have been replaced with a new one.

A few months later, I had a chance to go to that same theater on back-to-back days in October, which meant I would get in my horror movies! I saw *Smile 2* in their Dolby Cinema (also maintained separately from AMC by the Dolby team) and it was a fantastic experience. Colors were amazing, the picture quality was top notch, and the sound shook the theater and kept me on the edge of my seat. I have pretty solid equipment in my home theater, more than the average person, and I know I could not replicate that experience at home. It was simply awesome; this was exactly the experience I want when I go to a theater.

But the next day I went to support indie horror and bought a ticket to *Terrifier 3* in their standard theater. It was in auditorium one, right by the entrance, and based on past showings, it seemed like a popular theater for the bigger ticket sellers that the theater was showing. That is to say, it got a lot of foot traffic, had a lot of seating, and wasn't hidden in the back of the facility in a smaller section where things might slip by. Right when I walked in, I knew something was wrong. The screen had a maroon or possibly purple tint to it. As the trailers played, it was immediately apparent that something was wrong when each of the green splash screens before the trailers looked like a strange blue and purple mixture. I waited, because sometimes the trailer package could have had issues.

Maybe the file was corrupted or damaged in some way, and it was the same trailer package I had seen before *Smile 2* the night before. A couple sitting next to me was tuned into the possible issue as well, and one of them looked at me with the same confused skeptical look I probably had on my face and asked if I saw what they saw. "Something is wrong with the color, right?" I agreed, and he left to go tell someone so we could get ahead of the issue in case it continued. He came back before the trailers ended and mentioned that the employees were aware of the issue, but that there was nothing they could do. It had been this way for a while, and they asked AMC corporate for new parts and service help, but they did not have a timeline for replacement yet.

The choice was to take a refund and go back to my hotel or stick it out. I stuck it out, as did many others, but the experience sucked. It looked like Art the Clown was attacking a bunch of purple-skinned aliens. What should have been vibrant red, highly stylized blood looked more like he had cut into Barney and was spilling the dinosaur's purple blood across the floor.

But again, who is to blame for this? It isn't the local theater and its employees. AMC does not have a franchise system, so each theater is at the mercy of AMC corporate to get things fixed. We tried to talk to a teenage employee, but they were also running the ticket sales counter and scanning everyone into their showings. There was barely anyone working in this large twenty-screen theater. And even if they had the time to do it, they did not have the knowledge, resources, or equipment to fix anything. As they said, they had asked AMC corporate, and they got no help. When I posted about this experience online, without naming the theater, the comments came piling in. Many of the commenters immediately guessed this must have been an AMC theater. Others guessed it was a Regal or a Cinemark. One thing was for sure, they all knew it was a chain theater, because they had similar bad experiences in the past.

Although certain locations are better maintained than others, at this point I think it is fair to say that chain theaters are doing more harm than good for the movie theater experience. Many of them have outdated and aging equipment, and the cost of replacing bulbs is pushing theaters to dim their images to extend the life of the bulb well past the guidelines that the manufacturers would give. I have also experienced many blown speakers or subwoofers in theaters, where there is a distinct rattling sound throughout the film. And then, of course, there are the seats. Ten years ago, when all of the chain theaters started to remodel with new leather recliners, it was awesome. After ten years with little maintenance and care, it is not so awesome anymore. Seating with torn fabric is extremely common, as are recliners with broken mechanisms. It feels like there was a big push for chain theaters to deliver a more premium experience, which was successful, but with no plan for sustaining the experience as the facilities aged. At this point, I try to avoid any standard theater and opt for the Dolby Cinema or IMAX experiences that are maintained outside of the chain's control.

Aside from the technical issues, there is also a serious issue with theater etiquette. I don't know if COVID-19 broke everyone's brains or if smartphones and technology are to blame, but something has happened in the past few years that has made many frequent theater-goers second-guess going to the movies. I have heard from so many of my friends and followers online about the nightmares they are experiencing at their showings. There are people taking photos and videos during the movie to post on their Instagram story or Snapchat. There is a ton of loud talking with no regard for others. There are families bringing small children into R-rated movies because they don't want to pay for a babysitter.

It has become a total Wild West, and it spans across all generations, so I don't want anyone thinking I am blaming "the damn kids and their technology." I have had many experiences where people of my parents' generation are openly discussing the movie or asking their friends questions. The etiquette of the living room has made its way to the movie theater, and it is ruining the experience for the people who are there to actually watch the movie.

Thankfully, there are theaters like the aforementioned Drafthouse, where these things are monitored with real consequences. There is obviously some leeway, and the employees can take discretion, but if you have your phone out in a Drafthouse theater or talk loudly during the movie, they will ask you to leave. They also do not allow people to enter the theater after the movie start time, avoiding those distractions, and they do not allow children under five in the theater at any time unless it is a designated "family friendly" screening. Harsh? Maybe. But it works, and it is enforced. Drafthouse doesn't have ushers, but with their in-seat food and drink service, there is always someone in the theater monitoring the audience. The rules are simple, and people respect them or face consequences. I hate to have to treat adults like children, but that is what it has come to. The policies are a major reason why I would prefer to drive an hour to the Drafthouse theater in Boston than drive fifteen minutes to the chain theater down the road, and more theaters need to adopt similar practices because the behavior has gotten out of control.

Using Drafthouse as an example again of what a successful theater chain can look like, I love the emphasis they put on movie fans and generating unique experiences that will sell tickets. For example, in 2024, Drafthouse celebrated great movies with their "Time Capsule" programming series where they went back thirty, forty, and then fifty years in time, screening the classics from 1994, 1984, and 1974. They also host themed "movie parties," which their website describes as "an immersive, interactive experience for cinema fans featuring fun props, themed drinks, and more."

Also in Boston, there is a thriving local movie theater scene that includes venues like The Somerville Theatre, Coolidge Corner Theater, and The Brattle, which all have unique programming schedules. One of my favorites is the 70mm Film Festival at The Somerville Theatre each year, where I recently saw *2001: A Space Odyssey* screening from one of their rare 70mm prints. The experience was fantastic, with amazing picture quality and sound, an engaged and respectful audience, a short introduction from the theater, and even a proper intermission that allowed everyone to grab more snacks and another beer. I also fondly remember seeing *Jaws* at Coolidge Corner in 35mm. It was my wife's first time seeing *Jaws*, and the experience rocked. They had a contest for people to show off their best scars at the beginning of the screening, and it was so much fun to see *Jaws* on the big screen with an audience full of super fans.

More recently, I saw *Jaws* again on the big screen at an amazing independent theater, The Leavitt Theatre, in the beautiful seaside resort town of Ogunquit, Maine. Again, this theater offered an elevated movie experience that I was more than happy to pay for—tickets were cheap, but the food and drink are where you pay up. In the theater lobby is an award-winning cocktail bar where you can grab drinks before the movie starts. Once the doors open, the theater has standard seating, but it also has tons of small tables and unique seating areas as well as a bar and table service. The menu was excellent with tons of local food, and the staff was just as amazing with their attentiveness throughout the movie.

This was a more casual theater experience when it came to etiquette, but I didn't mind that. It was truly the best "dinner and a movie" date that my wife and I have been on, and it would also serve as a great model for the changes that theaters will need to make to survive streaming's dominance.

Finding these unique experiences and supporting the local theaters offering them up is truly the future of movie theaters in my opinion. I want to experience a full night out with good food, good drinks, comfortable seats, a fun atmosphere and pre-show buzz, and then a quality AV presentation of the film. Theaters have to go back to being theaters again rather than just screening rooms. They almost need to revert back to the 1940s mentality, making the movie theater an experience that you would want to dress up for rather than a throwaway thing to do on a Friday night, because they have lost that battle. The throwaway thing to do on a weekend night is to sit down and watch stuff on streaming apps or share social media videos with your friends and significant others. I fully expect that local repertory theaters and arthouse-style programming will keep these businesses open. Like physical media, movie theaters may become a niche experience again. Chains will continue to close and consolidate, which in theory is bad for accessibility to the theater, but that could open the door for more localized experiences and indie theaters having a renaissance of sorts.

If you love a world where movies feel like they used to, you have to go out and support these theaters and the films they show. You may not be able to see the latest Marvel movie, but I am telling you, seeing something like *Jaws* with a full audience in a summer beach town or watching *2001: A Space Odyssey* in 70mm with a packed crowd is worth more to me than seeing whatever the big new movie is. It feels like taking a trip back to a simpler time, and you know you will be surrounded by a respectful and invested audience who is there for the same reasons you are. And if you do want to see a new movie, check the local theaters and smaller regional chains. I have nothing against AMC or Cinemark or Regal, but the way to break this cycle is by supporting the smaller locations, and that is my plan for my personal theater experiences in the future. If it isn't a regional theater with local ownership, I do my best to avoid it if I can. I will happily pay more for a full-scale premium experience that goes to a business or nonprofit that has a goal of expanding the art of film instead of appeasing shareholders.

Outside of supporting physical media and finding better theatrical experiences, there are also ways to use the algorithms and modern technology to our advantage. Like everything else, social media is not inherently bad. It all comes down to how you use it. As someone who might be considered "chronically online," I have developed a few techniques that have helped me stay up to date on the latest in film news, filtering out the fluff and the noise from the content I want to see.

Since I have been in my beautiful little online algorithm for so long, I tend to forget that many others are struggling to find this information. There is so much junk out there. Facebook is flooded with AI posters and false announcements of new movies and TV shows that somehow still trick people every day. Some of my favorite websites from years past are now full of clickbait, "theories," speculation, and pure nonsense. It is hard to filter that out, but I have my methods, and I hope by sharing with you that you can also find some sort of happy medium in the age of digital consumption that allows you to get closer to that 2001 feeling.

First up, let's tackle social media and how to make the most of it. In the digital/social media age, humans can connect with anyone in the world in a matter of seconds. Anyone can post a video from their bedroom and have it potentially reach hundreds of millions of people. The opportunity is endless. If you stay focused on the positive side of social media and all the benefits that it provides versus all of the negativity, it is the best tool we have had in the history of humanity to connect with other people who have a shared interest. That is why I love social media. As much as I can be critical of the way that the platforms use our data and play against our best interests, if you can get beyond that, it is an amazing place, and it stretches far outside of an Instagram feed or TikTok

"For You Page." For someone who has a niche interest like music, movies, art, books, sports, woodworking, plumbing—it could be anything—the best place to look for connections on social media is typically outside of the biggest platforms.

In my eyes, Instagram, Facebook, YouTube, and TikTok all stand out as the highest level of social media. They have the most users, the most content, and by far the most annoying algorithms that want you to keep consuming their content no matter what. I find them the most useful as the place to cast a wide net and reach the maximum number of people. As a content creator, I am constantly throwing out new ideas and trying new types of content to reach new audiences. As a viewer, I am constantly bombarded with content that I am not interested in. It is a daily battle to wade through the shit and get to the gold. As annoying as that may be, it is a necessary evil.

You have to teach the algorithm what you want to see, and more importantly, what you don't want to see. They are finicky tools, and it only takes one or two clicks or fifteen-second videos to trigger the algorithm and tell it that you might be interested in that topic. It is no mistake that content creators that people "hate watch" and keep complaining about by leaving nasty comments will keep showing up in the video feeds with millions of views.

As far as the computer knows, people are watching the videos, opening the comments, leaving comments, and doing that multiple times. In the computer's eyes, these people have a ton of super fans who keep watching and engaging! It is true—no press is bad press.

Here is my challenge to you if you want an algorithm that feeds your interests and "listens." Go through the Explore tab or Discover tab or For You tab or whatever name the platforms each give to their Wild West of content. Scroll through as you usually do, but engage with stuff you like, and tell the algorithm when you come across stuff that you don't. All of the platforms have these features built in, but people rarely use them. In fact, Instagram has even been testing a "reset" button that will let you start fresh on the algorithm. But even then, you can ruin it just as quickly again if you don't follow these steps.

My advice is simple. Like the good videos that you enjoy, follow the accounts you want to hear more from, and take a quick pass on the stuff that is irrelevant or bothers you. Whatever you do, do not "hate watch" or leave nasty comments. For one, that sucks, and it doesn't make anyone feel good, you included. Secondly, it sends the wrong signals and you are guaranteed to get more junk like that on your feed. If you do that a few times and make a conscious effort to teach the platform what you want to see, you will see dramatic improvements quickly.

Instead of seeing a bunch of prank videos or the latest viral memes, you might be seeing posts from great industry accounts like Letterboxd, *The Hollywood Reporter*, *IndieWire*, The Academy of Motion Picture Arts and Sciences, The Criterion Collection, *Variety*, The AV Club, and more. You might be seeing videos from me or other reporters and creators who love film. You may discover smaller creators or other people who are simply fans and post their thoughts about movies online. You could find a new internet best friend.

So, don't be shy! Comment on these posts, and you will be surprised at how many replies you may get. Comment with a movie recommendation on someone else's post about a new movie they just watched and enjoyed. Make a new friend, make new connections, and I guarantee that you will find yourself transported right back to the line at the video store where people shared reviews and grew their cinematic interests through conversation.

Social media gives us this great opportunity, and as film fans, we need to do a better job of taking advantage of it and using it for good rather than bad. There are enough accounts that exist to do nothing but complain about movies. It's called "rage bait" and it is the worst part of the online movie community. It is so tiring to filter through videos making the dumb argument that a movie is "woke" or that a throwaway line in a *Star Wars* show broke the entire canon. My advice is to ignore those, focus on the positivity, find people who share interests with you, and don't be afraid to engage with creators who cover topics that you don't know as much about.

Some of the best conversations I have had on film have come with my friend Heath Holland, the man behind the *Cereal at Midnight* YouTube channel, podcast, and website. Heath knows infinitely more than I do about things like film noir, early horror movies, and the "golden age" of Hollywood. I would have never discovered a movie like *The Night of the Hunter* or a new creature feature from the '70s called *Tentacles* without Heath recommending those to me. In turn, I am sure I have made recommendations to him on things I may be into deeper than he is. And guess what—as much as we have talked and exchanged notes on many things, from film to family and content creation, I have (regrettably) never met Heath in person! But that is the beauty of the internet—I have a friend that I made online who lives a thousand miles away and keeps me on my toes when it comes to new movies I might have missed.

My friend Daisuke Beppu is another great example. I first noticed Daisuke on YouTube doing film reviews and talking about his extensive collection of Criterion Collection physical media releases. I got to know him more online, we did a few videos together, and eventually when he moved from Japan to Los Angeles just a couple of months before I had a trip out there, we got to meet up! I spent a couple of awesome hours with him in LA, grabbing lunch and buying movies at Amoeba Records, and he even dropped me off at the airport. I cherished those few hours and learned so much about movies. I got to walk around with him and he gave me recommendations on Westerns I should look into, a genre he knows a lot about, but I admittedly did not.

I have many other friends like this who I have met online, and some in person (shoutout to Adam Yeend, Adam Hlavac, Elliot Coen, Dominic Burgess, Ealan Osborne, Scott Neumyer, Ralph Potts, and many others) and it is a wonderful way to use social media for its most positive purpose: human connection. I don't have a ton of friends around me who share the same deep interest in movies, so social media has let me expand my horizons far beyond what I would have been exposed to in my day-to-day, IRL (in real life) journey. It is a fine line, because just like in life, it is all about the people you surround yourself with. If you surround yourself with negativity, you will experience that in heaps online. Luckily, I found a positive route, and by taking the time to build relationships with people beyond the comment section, I made amazing connections and discovered life-changing movies.

At that high level of social media, that was successful for me, and resulted in a lot of great conversations and expanded knowledge of film. The good news is, if that seems scary or you don't want to spend the time investing into those platforms, other places on the internet are less intimidating and overstimulating that also serve as great community gathering places for movie fans. For one, if you truly care about movies and finding new stuff to watch, you have to join Letterboxd. Letterboxd is social media, but it doesn't feel as overwhelming as most platforms. Essentially, it is a shared movie review platform. Users can create a free account to log their movies in a "diary," write reviews, rate movies on a scale from zero to five stars, and follow their friends to see their reviews and what they have been watching. You can see what is popular among the entire user base, but you can also see what is popular among your friends and followers. The nicest thing is, that even though there is an algorithm built in there somewhere, that the "trending" movies are always eclectic because of the user base.

Letterboxd has been growing steadily since 2020, starting as a fairly niche app with just over one million users and growing to a base of fourteen million users by June 2024.[96] However, even with that excellent growth, it is still a niche app for the most hardcore cinephiles with a lot less noise than other social media apps. For comparison's sake, keep in mind that Instagram has two billion users.[97] That's *billion*, with a "b." As much as I love Instagram, if you want a curated film-lover experience, Letterboxd is the clear winner.

A feature I enjoy on Letterboxd is their "List." So many creative lists are out there, and it is fun to browse through them all. For example, I have one called "Movies with Iconic Bandages"—think *Chinatown*, *Darkman*, *Eyes Without a Face*, and *The Invisible Man*—because I watched *Strange Darling* and thought, "Hm... I wonder how many other movies have really iconic bandages." So, I made a list. Outside of the weird and unique ones, there are also curated lists for reference, like the constantly updated "Top 250 Narrative Features" list run by the Letterboxd team based on user reviews, or lists based on feelings and

96 Kimberly Aguirre, "Letterboxd's Rise from Social Platform to Hollywood Powerhouse," *Los Angeles Times*, June 17, 2024. latimes.com/entertainment-arts/story/2024-06-17/letterboxd-rise-connecting-filmmakers-studios-audiences.

97 "Instagram Users: Statistics You Need to Know," Backlinko, last updated March 11, 2025, backlinko.com/instagram-users.

Lost in the Stream

emotions, like "Feeling Lost in Your 20s." If you search for a vibe, an emotion, a time period, a genre, an actor, a filmmaker, a film you like, or even for "movies with snowmen," there is most likely a list out there to give you more recommendations. From these lists, you can also add movies to your watch list, which is a perfect way to avoid endless scrolling and pick something from your own lists. It is an amazing tool, but I haven't even mentioned the best part—you get to see your completion percentage of the list!

As you log new movies in your diary, these lists will update with the percentage of the films on the list that you have watched. It gamifies the lists, but in a positive way. There is a sense of achievement if you can say you have seen all of the Top 250 on Letterboxd, and it is visible to others on the platform. I would compare it to something like earning an achievement in a video game, working to finish a game with 100 percent completion. It encourages you to watch more movies and complete the list. The next time you sit down to aimlessly scroll on streaming services, pop open Letterboxd, check your lists, and get 1 percent closer to completion. Trust me—it is a good feeling!

I also love Letterboxd for its simplicity. It is just movie posters, ratings, reviews, and writing about films. You can comment and like other reviews, and you can follow other users, but that is it. There isn't a ton of noise or unnecessary content. There are a few blogs each month from the Letterboxd team and they post informative videos and fun interviews on social media—I love the "What's Your Top 4" series, but that is not pushed in your face when using the app. You see movie posters and an article or two, and you can dive in without being distracted by other content. It is overwhelmingly positive and does not suffer from as much of the negativity that other platforms do, at least from what I have seen. If you want a fresh experience with a new social media app that won't become a time suck, Letterboxd is a great place to start. However, if you want something more adventurous, I recommend pairing up your Letterboxd usage with a community-based social media app like Reddit.

I know, Reddit can have a bad reputation. It has certainly had its fair share of controversies and bad user behavior. But the Reddit of 2015 is far different from the Reddit of today. While some may think it is for the worse, I have enjoyed it more as the communities have grown and added more moderation that keeps people on topic. If you are unfamiliar with Reddit, it is known as the "front page of the internet." Reddit is full of thousands of "subreddits" or "subs," which are user-moderated communities that discuss a specific topic. All subs are named in the same way: r/Music, r/Movies, r/Sports. The naming convention may seem odd at first, but you will get used to it. There is a subreddit for everything, from the most high-level topics like news, sports, and music to more specific subs that get into regional news, particular sports teams, and niche genres of music or certain artists.

While there is an r/Movies sub, I would stay away from the most generic subs like that. They are open season for all users and are loaded with negativity, shady advertising (movie studios are notorious for using Reddit communities and pretending to be regular people), and nonsense to filter through. The r/Movies has its place if you are looking for news on the biggest blockbusters and most mainstream films, but if you want something deeper with real discussion, that isn't the place for you.

Instead, you should find communities like r/Letterboxd, r/TrueFilm, r/Criterion, and r/Horror. If you want to dive deeper into physical media and get recommendations from other collectors, there are also subreddits for that at r/DVDCollection and r/4KBluray. Like I said, there is truly something for everyone.

My advice when it comes to Reddit is to curate your feed specifically to your interests. Reddit lives up to its "front page of the internet" tagline—there are thousands of subs with all kinds of information, both bad and good.

If you think that the news is depressing, Reddit is all of the world's news rolled into one community. Some people enjoy that to stay up to date, but if it is too much, you can leave those default communities or block their content. I highly recommend staying on your home page versus going to the "popular" or "explore" sections if you want to maintain a curated experience. Join the subs you are interested in and engage with them, and your feed will be full of relevant information. It is one of the most consistent social media platforms when it comes to that experience and even when they do try and push something "you might be interested in," it usually *is* interesting—a rare feat these days.

There are also hundreds of forums online where you could get similar interactions as Reddit, but I much prefer Reddit to traditional forums. For one, it is user-moderated. If someone leaves a nasty comment, users on Reddit can "downvote" it (basically like giving a thumbs down) and it will get hidden in favor of comments and posts that are "upvoted" (a thumbs up). With a traditional forum, you have to scroll through a lot of negativity or useless, off-topic posts. I quit using forums a few years back in favor of Reddit because of the constant negativity, and it has been one of the best choices I made for my movie-watching habits, finding new films, and above all else, my mental health. Reddit is no angel. It can do the same to your mental health if you let it. But if you stick to the communities I listed and contribute thoughtful comments and posts, I believe it will be a net positive. Reddit is the meeting place for like-minded folks across the world regardless of the topic or niche and it is one of the most powerful tools you can add to your arsenal to experience a journey through film that doesn't rely on the algorithm.

Social media can be used for good. There is a way to have positive experiences online and connect with other people in a way that makes you feel good. It takes a lot of effort, but it is possible with the right tools and approach. However, as great as social media may be for connecting with people across the world in the blink of an eye, nothing will ever replace human connection and conversation as the best way to discover new things. Even when I talk about meeting people on social media and connecting with them for years online, the most beneficial conversations I have had with them have been in person, or at the least over a video call. An hour of conversation is worth the same as years of social media back and forth in my eyes.

So, as scary as it may seem to connect with new people and strike up a conversation—trust me, I am riddled with social anxiety—it is so worth it. The next time you are at the movie theater and someone sits next to you, say hi. They are at the movies with you, so you already have a shared interest. Strike up the conversation and see what made them come to the theater. Maybe it will be because of a director they like, or an actor, or a writer. Maybe they just wanted to see something fun. Hell, maybe they give you a cold shoulder and want to be left alone—totally okay too! I have been there. But if you do start a friendly conversation while waiting for the movie, you may find yourself leaving with some new recommendations or recapping the film after it ends with your new friend for the night. Even if you never see them again, those simple connections are how people found new films and new interests before social media.

Another thing that I am starting to like more is the idea of a movie club. Book clubs are so popular for readers, with recent estimates putting the total number of Americans who participate in a book club at over five million. Most of these clubs are small, with ten or fewer members, but they are important connection points for book lovers to come together and share their love for reading. In my opinion, we should be doing the same thing for movies. I have a few friends online who live in Hollywood and have these get-togethers that make me jealous. But there is no reason you need to be in Hollywood to make this happen. You can pick a movie each month, gather a few cinephile friends, and come together to discuss the movie in-depth. During a natural conversation about one movie, you know that dozens and dozens of others will be mentioned, which makes for a perfect environment to build a new list of recommendations to watch.

No matter how you want to break free from the algorithm, there are plenty of options. Scrolling through Netflix or Prime Video is not necessary in the wide world of information that we live in. Use apps like Letterboxd to create and curate watch lists. Use social media like Instagram to connect with creators and industry accounts that will keep you up to date on all the latest in film. Use Reddit to express your thoughts on film and engage in deep discussions—and plenty of memes and fun as well. And, of course, talk to people. We only choose the algorithm because it is easy and mindless. It requires no effort to click a button on your remote, open Netflix, and choose whatever they have trending or "recommended for you." At the end of a long day, sometimes that feels good. But it feeds into the mentality and systems that I think are trying their best to kill creativity and the movies that we want to see by giving us the easy option instead. So, buck convenience every now and then and get outside the algorithm. You will thank your past self for doing it, I guarantee it.

CONCLUSION

THE FUTURE OF MOVIES: WHAT CHANGES ARE COMING NEXT?

We live in a convenient world, which certainly makes life easier than a settler from the 1800s trying to find food to survive. It is nice to not have to worry about those things and live an easier life. For many industries and communities, this is a huge net positive. But in the world of film and art as a whole, I do not see it as such a positive. This world of convenience and easy living is slowly turning the world into a *Wall-E* or *Idiocracy* situation, where art and education are devalued, convenience has made us all lazy, and we don't seek new experiences. I hope that terrifies you as much as it terrifies me. Without people who are driven to explore new avenues in the arts, the world becomes boring and predictable.

The problem is that this is what a capitalist society loves. They love boring and predictable things because risk is scary—hence why movies from established IPs are the only ones being pushed by the major studios. They don't want to take risks. They would rather make another poorly received franchise movie, knowing that it will still make them millions on name alone than try something new and potentially lose, even though the upside could be much higher. As much as industry heads across the world speak about innovation and technology, those changes are all in an effort to get people more comfortable and brainless, consuming everything thrown at them for the sake of convenience.

When people are trained to drop their critical thinking skills every day, they are also being trained to reject anything that their brain finds to be difficult. A more challenging movie like *Tenet* or *The Game* or *2001: A Space Odyssey* will be deemed "boring" by audiences who refuse to think critically and want easier entertainment. I see it all the time in comments on my social media posts when I recommend great films, especially anything older than ten or twenty years. The comments like "It's too slow," "Boring," "I fell asleep," "This movie sucks" are common. Any art form is subjective and people are certainly entitled to their opinions, but I have to believe that the rise of streaming and easy access to mindless entertainment has only made people less tolerant of the challenge of watching a movie that deserves full attention.

In a recent interview, actor Willem Dafoe, well-known for starring in challenging films, said something that I think encapsulates exactly the way I am feeling right now as well:[98]

98   Zack Sharf, "Willem Dafoe: 'Challenging Movies' Don't Do Well on Streaming Because 'People Go Home' and Say 'Let's Watch Something Stupid Tonight,'" *Variety*, January 9, 2024, variety.com/2024/film/news/willem-dafoe-streaming-kills-challenging-films-1235866060.

The kind of attention that people give at home isn't the same. More difficult movies, more challenging movies, cannot do as well when you don't have an audience that's really paying attention. That's a big thing. I miss the social thing of where movies fit in the world. You go see a movie, you go out to dinner, you talk about it later, and that spreads out. People now go home, they say, "Hey, honey, let's watch something stupid tonight," and they flip through and they watch five minutes of ten movies, and they say, "Forget it, let's go to bed." Where's that discourse found?

Dafoe hits the nail on the head. I find myself doing it some nights. But you have to find the time to challenge yourself and work out those brain muscles as well. Not every movie will appeal to you, and you will find some are a miss for your tastes and interests. But that is also a critical part of how you find your groove and discover what works for you and what doesn't.

However, the streaming services are embracing this lack of focus and attention and telling filmmakers to adjust scripts based on the feedback and research they are getting that is telling them most people are "watching" movies while scrolling on their phones. Netflix has become a weird type of "second screen" content, where it is essentially background noise to the audience's focus on their social media apps or mobile games. Movies are something you put on to have "something to watch" rather than making an investment into the full film.

Writer Will Tavlin has a great essay in the January 2025 edition of *N+1* magazine titled "Casual Viewing," where he dissects the current state of film and Netflix's impact in particular. Tavlin's essay speaks to a lot of the issues with Netflix and how it has adapted to adjust for higher earnings and shareholder happiness, including revealing research into how Netflix names its films for search engines. It is an incredibly well-written essay well worth your time and would make for a great companion to this book. One of the most revealing parts of the essay is the way in which Netflix films are written, with dialogue that so explicitly lays out what is happening and is meant for people not watching the movie so they can keep up on the audio alone. Here is an excerpt from the essay which I think is the most damning evidence against the current model of filmmaking for streaming:[99]

99   Will Tavlin, "Casual Viewing: Why Netflix Looks Like That," *n+1*, 2025, nplusonemag.com/issue-49/essays/casual-viewing.

Lost in the Stream

> *Slipshod filmmaking works for the streaming model, since audiences at home are often barely paying attention. Several screenwriters who've worked for the streamer told me a common note from company executives is, "Have this character announce what they're doing so that viewers who have this program on in the background can follow along." ("We spent a day together," Lohan tells her lover, James, in Irish Wish. "I admit it was a beautiful day filled with dramatic vistas and romantic rain, but that doesn't give you the right to question my life choices. Tomorrow I'm marrying Paul Kennedy." "Fine," he responds. "That will be the last you see of me because after this job is over I'm off to Bolivia to photograph an endangered tree lizard.")*

My criticism, and Dafoe's, is not meant to be levied at any single genre, streaming service, studio, or filmmaker. There are plenty of incredible superhero movies, action movies, horror movies, streaming exclusive movies, comedies, thrillers, and more. I don't want to sound elitist or snobby—I will gladly watch *Jackass 3* or *Scary Movie* or *Grandma's Boy* and just sit back and relax. I love the influx of true crime documentaries and things of that nature that are all over streaming services now. I immensely enjoyed films like *No One Will Save You* (Hulu Exclusive), *The Killer* (Netflix Exclusive), and *Apartment 7A* (Paramount+ Exclusive). A movie on streaming or a genre like comedy or superhero movies does not automatically mean that the movie is not worth watching or is "brainless."

But the truth is that more often than not these days, that is how the biggest mainstream movies are made, especially those designed for streaming. They are made for mass appeal and a lack of focus. Look at an action movie star from the '80s or '90s like Arnold Schwarzenegger. Arnold did *Commando*, *Predator*, *The Terminator*, *Total Recall*, *The Running Man*, *Red Heat*, *Conan*, and *True Lies*. Compare that to the most recent action stars—Keanu Reeves, for example. I love Keanu, and he makes great movies. But his list is a lot more sequel-heavy, like *John Wick* and its three sequels and *The Matrix* and that franchise's three sequels. Chris Hemsworth is another action star who could have had a run like Arnold, but he has been busy playing Thor for almost fifteen years now. Arnold's resume is more impressive to me because the movies were all original. They were new characters, new scripts, new stories—all the things that are lacking in modern Hollywood. Even in what some film snobs would consider a "brainless" genre like action (I am not one of them—bring on the action movies), the differences between the Hollywood of old and the new regime are stark.

As filmmaking is challenged by tools like artificial intelligence in the future, the fight for convenience over quality becomes even more difficult. Entire AI "studios" are being built in the tech industry right now, promising to "revolutionize Hollywood" by taking the humans out of the equation and working with "generative AI artists." Just the phrase "generative AI artists" is so backward that it makes me want to throw up. Generative AI only generates inputs that it is given, so these "artists" are just good at plagiarizing other people's work to turn it into something new. I'm not sure it takes much skill or effort to say, "Write me a script for a new movie that tells the origin story of (insert franchise character here)." With so many inputs from books, other movies, comics, TV shows, and all other available media, it would probably take a good AI system a few minutes to write a feature-length script for just about any franchise character out there.

AI-written scripts are bad enough, but that is just words on paper. The next step these tech companies want to take is making the entire movie in AI, from the writing to the acting or animation. I can't even imagine what these soulless atrocities might look like, and I know that I have absolutely no interest in them. But once again,

Hollywood is run by capitalists and exists in a system that is now run entirely by dollars over passion, so it is almost inevitable that these movies will be made. If you thought Netflix giving Jake Paul and a geriatric Mike Tyson a platform was a waste of time, just remember that that nonsensical event drew in sixty million viewers. Seeing that success, you bet that Netflix and other streaming services will have no issue greenlighting AI projects and cheap productions that lack any humanity. They are doing it now and global audiences are tuning in, so what will stop them in the future?

The defenders of AI in movies and art will claim that it "democratizes" the movie-making experience. With AI, anyone can "write" a script or "make" a movie. You can take the crazy ideas that you have in your dreams and make them a reality. Now don't get me wrong, I fully stand behind giving more people access to the tools and systems that will help them get their movies made. I know there are underprivileged and underrepresented people who have the chops and the creativity to be great but don't have the resources. But I am not behind giving that access and ability to just anyone so that some lazy guy in his basement can make a *Star Wars* movie without any female characters so it isn't "woke" anymore. We all know that is what will happen, and that is a disaster for the art form of film.

The simple fact is that not everyone should be making movies. If we can all do it, then what makes one movie special over another? It cheapens the entire industry, even more than all of the greenlit streaming projects are already doing. In the wide world we live in, some people are special and creative and deserve to have their projects made. Most of us, unfortunately, are not. And that's okay. If we had a million Picassos running around, Picasso wouldn't be special.

I am a firm believer that there is something more than just tools and resources when it comes to filmmaking. Human experiences have shaped our greatest filmmakers. Special intangibles can't be developed with AI. But regardless of how I, and I am sure many of you, feel, the capitalist system that is Hollywood will feel the opposite. They want films to be made for pennies so that they can make billions. AI will help them reduce costs, but it won't all come at once. They know audiences would reject AI films right away, so they will take their time transitioning. It started a few years back when they built models of actors who passed away, like Carrie Fisher in *Rogue One*. Soon enough, AI will take over some of the artistic elements, replacing the CGI artists and visual effects teams that can be costly. Then you will see scripts edited by AI, or smaller productions and TV shows edited by AI film editing software. Eventually, there will be 100 percent

AI-created scripts, AI actors and actresses designed to act and talk like real people, and finally, completely artificial films.

Artificial intelligence has its place in the world. I use it in my day-to-day work, and it allows a one-man content creation business like mine to expand capabilities in a way that would not have been possible even a few years ago. But I also pay artists and video editors and other skilled labor jobs that I require from time to time. I use AI to make monotonous tasks easier to accomplish and to enhance my work or give me three heads when I only have one. But rest assured, I have not used AI in writing this book, and my publisher has not either. Writing, like film, should also come from a human brain.

Are we screwed? Maybe. But not if we vote with our wallets and use our voices as the consumer. Capitalism only works when consumers do what they do best: consume. If we reject these projects, starting with even the smallest introductions of AI, then the profits won't be there. Voting with our wallets is the most important thing that we can do to stop this "revolution" from occurring. If you think film is in a strange place now with all of the algorithms and formulas driving the content that is produced, wait until humans are removed from the equation completely. That is a world I do not want to live in, and a world I will not participate in. I know there will still be those who make movies how they are supposed to be made—with humans—and those are the creators who I will support. I would urge you to do the same, or this snowball effect of algorithms and pure capitalist greed currently running Hollywood will only grow larger and larger until eventually, it can't be stopped and buries us all.

Ultimately, the future of Hollywood, movies, and entertainment as a whole all comes down to us, the audience. We are in control of what we want to see, and we have the power to direct corporations where we want them to go. In the 2010s, I think we all got complacent. We were excited by the prospect of *The Avengers* and *Batman vs. Superman* and all of the cool things that could be done in a new age of franchise movies and multiverses. I was swept up in it, too. It was a great time to be a fan of movies—until it got boring.

What I have seen so far in the 2020s has encouraged me more than discouraged me. Audiences are looking for something more in their entertainment and they are searching for original ideas, whether from a franchise or not. Name recognition and audience buy-in are huge, hence why sequels, reboots, and franchise films will continue to dominate Hollywood. But I have hope that they will have to be better than they have been in the past as audiences reject the lazy storytelling we have been subjected to in the last few years. You can only watch so many movies about superheroes saving the world from some supernatural power that comes from another planet and rains down terror from the skies. It has been the same formula over and over again, and I believe audiences are finally beginning to reject it.

Now, we are seeing a shift with films like *Prey*, one of the biggest hits of 2022 because it offered a wholly original and unique take on a franchise that had dried up after a few terrible sequels and reboots. *Nosferatu* is not an original film—it has been made multiple times—but Robert Eggers is giving it a fresh coat of paint and bringing his trademark style to the film. *Evil Dead Rise* took the *Evil Dead* franchise, moved it to the city, introduced a new set of characters, and made for a film that was a blast to watch. *The Batman* was another incredible film that felt completely original even though it featured a character who has been on screen for decades. The "Detective Batman" approach that Matt Reeves took was different from anything we had seen from this character, making a *Silence of the Lambs/Batman* hybrid movie that blew me away. Even going back to *Rogue One: A Star Wars Story*— in my opinion, the best of all the *Star Wars* films since

Disney took over—you can see what an original take on existing material can look like if it is done right.

Sequels are here to stay. Franchises are here to stay. Reboots will keep coming. But if the approach follows the trends I have been seeing recently, I don't see any issue with those films. They might as well be independent movies simply using the name recognition of a popular character or franchise to get funded. But they offer a fresh perspective and give us something new, even if they do fit into the current Hollywood system. The more that films like those can be successful, the more chance there is for new characters and stories to be developed. Every one of these films started with a young director creating a masterpiece that spawned a franchise, so I am always looking to see who might be next.

At the end of the day, what the future holds for movies is up to you. What you consume and how you consume it will shape the way Hollywood responds. The studios and streaming services are capturing hundreds of data points on you every day. Your actions and response to change directly impact their next move. If you want to see more original films, buy tickets to more original films. If you want to see more science fiction, buy tickets to science fiction films. If you want to see streaming services improve their offering, cancel your subscription and move to another service that better fits your needs, or better yet, buy some physical media. It does seem like such a simple proposition, but the only way to truly find movies outside the algorithm and improve your connection with film is to make those choices yourself. I can try to convince you and preach about the importance of getting off the streaming apps and using other tools to discover new films, but nothing matters unless you do something about it.

I have faith in the change coming, and I hope that you do too. Hopefully this book helps others to make the changes in their movie-watching habits that I believe will lead to a happier journey through film. Hopefully it helps everyone to break free from the algorithm bubble and dive into some of the thousands of amazing films not being recommended by streaming services and social media every day. If this changes even one person's thinking about how they approach their media consumption, I will be a happy guy.

If there is one takeaway, remember that your wallet is the most important tool you have to make a change in the world. It is more important than your vote in any election. It is far more important than a social media post complaining about the current state of affairs. It is more important than this book or any other talking head and their opinions, regardless of how many people they reach. Money makes the world go round, and we are all at the wheel. So, let's make it the best world we can, filled with original storytelling, incredible visual masterpieces, and above all else, human connection.

ACKNOWLEDGMENTS

This book wouldn't be possible without a collection of people. First and foremost, my wife, Coryana. I couldn't do any of this without you. Thank you for always being at my side since we were just kids—look at us now! Your support through late nights spent writing and being an amazing mother to our kids is what made this book possible.

To my parents, Keith and Maura. Thank you for always supporting me, no matter what. You are amazing parents and incredible grandparents, and you taught me so much. This book wouldn't exist without you meticulously editing my school papers with me and making me a better writer. I am so happy that I can add my book to Dad's collection!

To my uncle Doug, who pushed me into a new world of film as a young adult and fueled my passion. Thank you for always being a positive influence in my life, and of course, taking me to so many movies!

To my publisher, Mango Publishing, and my editors, Naomi Shammash and Hugo Villabona. Thank you for your patience and guidance in helping my words reach so many people.

ABOUT THE
Author

J eff Rauseo was born in Massachusetts and now lives in southern New Hampshire with his wife, Coryana, and their two children, Sam and Hannah. A lifelong movie enthusiast, he has been creating content online about his passion for film and physical media since 2015. *Lost in the Stream* is his debut book. He has a bachelor's in political science from the University of Massachusetts Lowell. When he isn't watching movies or creating content, he works in digital marketing.

Mango Publishing, established in 2014, publishes an eclectic list of books by diverse authors—both new and established voices—on topics ranging from business, personal growth, women's empowerment, LGBTQ+ studies, health, and spirituality to history, popular culture, time management, decluttering, lifestyle, mental wellness, aging, and sustainable living. We were named 2019 and 2020's #1 fastest growing independent publisher by Publishers Weekly. Our success is driven by our main goal, which is to publish high-quality books that will entertain readers as well as make a positive difference in their lives.

Our readers are our most important resource; we value your input, suggestions, and ideas. We'd love to hear from you—after all, we are publishing books for you!

Please stay in touch with us and follow us at:

Facebook: Mango Publishing

Twitter: @MangoPublishing

Instagram: @MangoPublishing

LinkedIn: Mango Publishing

Pinterest: Mango Publishing

Newsletter: mangopublishinggroup.com/newsletter

Join us on Mango's journey to reinvent publishing, one book at a time.

www.ingramcontent.com/pod-product-compliance
Lightning Source LLC
Jackson TN
JSHW030937120825
89226JS00002B/2